THE
CURRENCY OF LOVE

THE
CURRENCY OF LOVE

A Courageous Journey to Finding

the Love Within

JILL DODD

ENLIVEN BOOKS
—
ATRIA

NEW YORK   LONDON   TORONTO   SYDNEY   NEW DELHI

ENLIVEN
ATRIA

An Imprint of Simon & Schuster, Inc.
1230 Avenue of the Americas
New York, NY 10020

First Enliven Books / Atria Books hardcover edition June 2017

ENLIVEN BOOKS / ATRIA BOOKS and colophon are trademarks of
Simon & Schuster, Inc.

For information about special discounts for bulk purchases, please
contact Simon & Schuster Special Sales at 1-866-506-1949 or
business@simonandschuster.com.

The Simon & Schuster Speakers Bureau can bring authors to your live event. For
more information or to book an event, contact the Simon & Schuster Speakers
Bureau at 1-866-248-3049 or visit our website at www.simonspeakers.com.

Interior design by Kyoko Watanabe

Manufactured in the United States of America

10 9 8 7 6 5 4 3 2 1

Library of Congress Cataloging-in-Publication Data

Names: Dodd, Jill, author.
Title: The currency of love : a courageous journey to finding the love within / Jill Dodd.
Description: New York : Enliven Books/Atria, [2017]
Identifiers: LCCN 2016052178 (print) | LCCN 2017010976 (ebook) | ISBN
  9781501150371 (hardcover) | ISBN 9781501150388 (pbk.) | ISBN 9781501150395
  (eBook)
Subjects: LCSH: Dodd, Jill. | Models (Persons)—United States—Biography.
Classification: LCC HD8039.M772 U5367 2017 (print) | LCC HD8039.M772
(ebook) | DDC 746.9/2092 [B] —dc23
LC record available at https://lccn.loc.gov/2016052178

ISBN 978-1-5011-5037-1
ISBN 978-1-5011-5039-5 (ebook)

For Natalie and Stella

CONTENTS

AUTHOR'S NOTE

While writing this book, I referenced the hundreds of letters I wrote from Paris to my family and friends. I also relied on journals I kept during the time period of the book. My other source of memory is the thousands of photos, both personal and professional, that bring me right back to the moments when all of this happened. I researched news articles when necessary to find exact dates and other details. Some of the main characters were gracious enough to read my manuscript to be sure the story felt authentic to them. I changed some names and identifying details of people portrayed in the book. In some cases, I chose not to include people and events in an effort to keep the story focused and concise.

THE
CURRENCY OF LOVE

I'm always happy by the sea

PIRATES

August 1980, Cannes, France

Earth crunches under the tires as we roll to a stop. "We're here!" Dominic shouts. All five of us pile out in the dark and wander instinctively toward the music and twinkling lights. I see a huge fire in the distance.

"Where are we?" I ask. Pepper body-slams me, singing in drunken French. We're both a bit wobbly from drinks earlier at the pool and the champagne in the limo. I balance on the balls of my feet so I don't trip in my heels. I'm charged up and happy about finally being on vacation.

Dominic puts his hand around my waist. "Jill, this is the famous old Le Pirate, come on!"

The closer we get, the louder the music becomes. I can't believe my eyes—I see hordes of long-haired, tattooed, shirtless pirates, banging tambourines and strumming guitars. A twenty-foot bonfire crackles, lighting up the night sky. Overhead, more pirates climb ropes with daggers clinched between their teeth. It looks like a scene out of *Pirates of the Caribbean*, except the movie hasn't been made yet.

A long table sparkles with candles, crystal, and silver. At the head sits a young Egyptian-looking girl with dark, exotic eyes and jet-black hair. Her blue, beaded dress shimmers in the candlelight. Sophisticated men and women animatedly converse. In the past, I might have felt out of place, but after modeling in Paris for a year, I can fit in anywhere. Suddenly, a suited man stands up and hurls his champagne glass into the fire. Another guy throws his on the rocks and shards of glass ricochet. Adrenaline rushes through me as pandemonium breaks out. Of course, I jump right in. "I love this place!" I scream to Pepper. "It's better than the Greek restaurants in Saint-Germain!"

"Hollywood doesn't have places like this, I bet!" she yells back to me.

A dark-tanned, greasy old pirate hands us each a glass of champagne. "*Salute!*" I take a swig, and another pirate pulls out my chair. Dominic begins introducing the other guests at the table, which is futile with the thundering music. I shake hands, nod, and smile anyway.

Pirates serve plates of baked potatoes topped with sour cream and caviar. I have never tasted caviar before and pucker at the salty tang. I gulp the champagne and hurl the glass into the fire. A pirate promptly brings me another. As the Spanish guitars, tambourines, and drums speed up, I want to dance, not eat, so I jump up and throw my plate in the fire.

In the midst of this frenzy, I turn back around and notice a man watching me, smiling, laughing slightly. Normally, this would be creepy, but it's not. I smile back and sit down. He brings his chair next to mine. He kind of reminds me of my friend's dad, who I danced with at a wedding. I'm grateful that he's not some young guy who is going to try to sleep with me. He is shorter than me, broad-chested, and balding, which makes me feel in control of the situation.

I can't hear a word he's saying, so he takes my hands and pulls me up to dance. We twirl all around the dusty ground together until he stops and grabs a chair, tossing it into the fire. We watch as the blaze envelops the charred skeleton. He smiles at me, which I take as a challenge and throw one in too. We look at each other, laughing, and slam together again tight, like two magnets, whirling around to the wild gypsy music in front of the flames.

It's only us dancing. Everyone else is drinking, eating, and laughing at the festive table, providing a pretty backdrop for our little world. Musicians circle us again, and he and a pirate grab my hands and feet, scoop me up, and swing me back and forth like a rag doll. I let my head fall back with my hair grazing the dirt, watching the flames from upside down. I am totally surrendered to the spirit of the party, euphoric with freedom.

They lower me to the ground, and I stagger to the table. The older man with the huge smile helps me into my chair, but remains standing, watching me. Then he sits down slowly, leaning slightly toward my face, his eyes locked on mine. We sit looking at each other and start laughing again. His sparkling eyes are full of life. Then he tenderly pulls my left arm, palm up, onto the table, pushes my sleeve up, and writes *I love you*, in blood, down my forearm. It takes me a moment to realize it's blood. I'm stunned, but I like it. It feels like we've made some kind of secret pact.

A pirate sees the blood and whisks him away for a bandage. Pepper's off socializing somewhere as I sit at the crowded table among the partying, laughing guests, trying to take in what just happened. I'm lost in my own world, dizzy-drunk and surrounded by strangers in this mad place. All I can do is stare at my arm. Time stands still as my heart soars overhead like a bird. I like that he wrote *I love you*. I don't wipe it off.

I don't know who he is, but over the next two years I will know him intimately. He is Adnan Khashoggi, the billionaire Saudi Arabian arms dealer.

First professional shoot in Hollywood, 1978

WILHELMINA MODELS

1979, Century City

Wilhelmina Cooper, or "Willy," sits across from me at her desk, smoking and thumbing through my portfolio. The living legend and namesake of my agency, Wilhelmina Models, has traveled from New York City to Los Angeles to meet her West Coast girls.

Because of her reputation as a glamorous New York model in the sixties, I had built her up in my mind as a great beauty, statuesque and elegant. But the frail woman in front of me is gaunt, her complexion powdery and gray. She's cold and reserved—not an ounce of warmth or personality. Maybe New York does that to people. I want to connect with her, but it's clearly not happening.

"So Jill, you need to lose ten pounds. Grow your hair out long—no bangs." She wags her fingers that hold the cigarette at me. "Your nails should be long and manicured—always," she says, taking a drag.

"But my nails are so thin, they don't grow long. I teach swimming lessons and they get all soggy."

She's not interested. "Get acrylics, then. You could do a lot of swim and lingerie. I think you need some time in Paris. I'll call our French agent. It was nice to meet you." She hands back my portfolio, we shake hands, and I walk out, deflated.

The head of my agency thinks I'm fat and doesn't like my hair. Apparently, one hundred and twenty-three pounds is way too heavy for my five-foot-nine frame, and how am I supposed to instantly grow long hair? It'll take years!

Right then, my world goes small and dark into a tunnel of self-disgust. I'm a fool to think I can make it as a model in New York!

On my way through the parking garage, I think of ways to starve myself. I drive in a daze to the nail salon, where the manicurist layers on toxic epoxy and grinds it with an electric sander. My mind ping-pongs between bad ideas, self-abusing thoughts, and terrible ways to push down my hunger.

I hate these fake nails. They make me feel claustrophobic, like I can't breathe, so I rip them off with wire cutters the night before leaving for Paris.

Paris parking lot, winter 1980

FRENCH FOR TRAVELERS

February 1980, LAX to Charles de Gaulle

The girl sitting next to me is a model. I can tell from her ridiculously beautiful, perfect face. I assume she's on her way to model in Paris like me. "Hi, I'm Jill. Who are you with?"

"I'm with Willy—you?" Her blue eyes and puffy lips are totally marketable and, with that long, chocolate-brown hair, she'll have no problem. I wish mine were long like that.

"I am too, but I've never seen you at the agency. Sorry, what's your name?"

"Scarlett—I just moved from Portland. That's why you haven't seen me."

The plane ascends and the cabin fills with cigarette smoke, giving me an instant pounding headache. I look at Scarlett. "You don't smoke, do you?"

"No! It's horrible—I can't breathe." She waves her hand, trying to clear the smoky fog in front of her face.

"Wait, are you going to work with Paris Planning? Have you met Gerald?" I ask.

"Yeah, I met him in LA. I think we're staying together in the same hotel."

9

"Good! I'm glad we don't have to do this alone."

"You know Gerald only chose two girls from the whole US to come to Paris, right?" she says.

"No. Really?" I feel instantly flattered, but wonder if it's really true.

I grab my *French for Travelers* book from my bag. I need to know how to say "hello," "please," and "thank you." Scarlett buries her nose in a romance novel with a sexy woman and a hunky man on the cover.

Everybody tried to talk me out of going to Paris except the agency and Alleen, who prepared me with "Lambchop, the best way I can describe the French is that if there's a goddamn pipe in the room, they'll wallpaper it. They have a genetic need to decorate everything. Oh, and it's cold as fuck there in the winter. I mean it, Choppers, if you go to Paris in the winter, you'll freeze your ass off."

Alleen is a realist. And yes, it's winter—February to be exact. Alleen is the only person I know who's been to Paris, and I'm nervous—and not just about the weather. I'm on a mission to support myself financially, and my need for freedom and independence is stronger than the fear knocking at me. Besides, I'm an expert at silencing fear and stuffing down anxiety until I can't even feel it. I'm gonna make it on my own. I have to. I'm determined to never depend on anyone ever again. I've got to be free. I absolutely must be able to support myself financially and create my own life on my own terms.

After eleven hours and no sleep, we land after midnight at Charles de Gaulle airport, which has the modern esthetic of Tomorrowland at Disneyland. People from foreign countries I can't even imagine sleep in piles on the floor.

We drag our heavy, overstuffed suitcases past them all into the RER train car that takes us to the center of Paris. Whizzing along in the dark tunnel, I look at Scarlett through my bloodshot haze. "I'm not staying here more than a month, two at the most."

"Same."

Our train screeches to a halt. We get off and wander in the dim underground Metro maze under Paris.

"What does *sortie* mean?" Scarlett says, looking up.

"I don't know," I say, agitated. We drag our huge bags through tunnel after tunnel, up and down a thousand stairs, trying to budge every locked turnstile and stainless-steel door. The Metro is closed for the night, and we're locked in. I stand in front of a pair of steel doors, determined to get over them, and look back at the no-way-in-hell look on Scarlett's face.

"Come on, I'll help you over," I beg. I hadn't noticed how tiny she is, maybe only five-four. She rolls her eyes and finally climbs on the ticket-sucking part of the turnstile, then throws a leg over the top of the steel door and slides down the opposite side. I hoist the luggage up and over, climb up, and jump down.

We wander through what feels like miles of tunnels and thousands of steps until we hear the echo of cars speeding on the wet street above. After climbing one last flight of stairs, hauling our heavy bags up one stair at a time, we're finally outside. Like Alleen said, Paris is cold as fuck—rainy and windy too.

Soon, a taxi spots us waving in the dark, and we hand the driver the address. "*Ah oui, Saint-Germain.* He jumps out and stuffs our suitcases in his trunk. "*Allez, les filles, allons-y!*" We climb in and he steps on the gas.

Racing through its streets, Paris's absolute beauty snaps me out of my sleepy, frustrated crankiness and takes me in her grip. We turn a corner, and through the mist I see the tree-lined Seine glowing dark black, twinkling with reflections of streetlights and bridges. Grand palaces are lit up on either side. It's pure magnificence, and it makes downtown Los Angeles look like the apocalypse.

The taxi drops us at the hotel the French agency has booked for us. The door is locked so we push the buzzer. The thick, wood slab opens with a thud to a disheveled man, half asleep in his pajamas. He motions for us to follow, and we drag our bags up four flights of creaky stairs to the tiny room with one small bed, a bidet, and sink—no toilet. The man disappears and we collapse into bed and turn out the light.

"How old are you, Jill?" Scarlett asks quietly.

"I just turned twenty, in October."

"Can you keep a secret?" she asks.

"Yeah, of course."

"I lied to the agency. I'm not twenty-one."

I look up in the dark, at the ceiling. "Oh. Well, how old are you?"

"How old do I look?" She sounds tentative.

"I don't know, like twenty-four? I'm guessing high."

"Nope. I'm twenty-eight and barely five-four. I'm so scared to be here. When I met Gerald we were sitting down. I do mostly face and hair stuff, but still, I don't think this is gonna work. Do you think they're gonna send me home?"

"First of all, you don't look anywhere near twenty-eight and you're so pretty, you're gonna do great. I can totally see you killin' it with that face of yours. Hopefully, we both will."

Paris street, winter 1980

MY PLAN DE PARIS

European police sirens and honking cars pull me out of my coma in the morning. It's so cold my face is numb. Out of the corner of my eye, I see a pipe that runs along the wall. It's covered in faded floral wallpaper, like the walls. I smile and think about Alleen.

The city glistens in the morning fog as our taxi speeds over Pont Neuf and up rue de Rivoli. Paris Planning is at 29 rue Tronchet, with the La Madeleine church on one end of the street and Galeries Lafayette at the other. A huge wooden door opens onto a cobblestone courtyard and we climb the old stairway to the second floor where a shiny brass plaque on the door reads PARIS PLANNING MODELS.

We open the door to pounding club music, ringing phones, and yelling in French. The stark white, modern, calm-looking space is anything but calm. Loud, fast-talking agents are manning phones behind a chest-high counter running the length of the slim room, and opposite them is a wall of windows and shelves stacked with model composites. Each composite, or card, has fashion, head, and body shots with the model's name, measurements, and the Paris Planning logo, like an auction house or real estate office.

Gerald, the head of Paris Planning, bounces down to greet us with a huge smile. *"Bonjour les filles*, I see you made it to Paris! How was your sleep? You girls ready to work?"

His French accent is thick. He kisses us on both cheeks. Gerald is more handsome than I remember. He's confident, even cocky, but somehow it suits him and looks natural. Even his crooked, tobacco-stained teeth look cool. Messy brown curls fall around his face and smile lines frame a naughty grin and blue eyes. I thought black leather pants and biker jackets were only for rock stars. This is no longer true.

"Here are your bookers." He gestures toward the counter. "You have Evelyn, Isabel, Jacqueline, and last but not least, Pepper." Her desk is on the end. She leans over to shake our hands, a phone to her ear, pen in her mouth. "*Bonjour,* ladies," she purrs in a husky exaggerated accent.

Gerald continues, "Your mailboxes are there, and just past is the men's agency, Francois Lano. Pepper will give you your list of go-sees. Any questions, speak to her. I'll see you later." He kisses our cheeks and returns to his station.

Pepper lowers her eyelids halfway. "Give me your books, girls." This time she's speaking with an American southern drawl. She's petite with brown hair, blue eyes, and an inflated-looking pug nose, which you'd think would be ugly, but somehow looks sexy. She wears an off-the-shoulder green sweater, a tight black skirt, fishnets, and heels. I love her makeup—black liquid eyeliner, matte red lips.

She's examining my portfolio when, to my shock, she starts pulling out all my best work. She hands me a new white Paris Planning portfolio with only four shots in the plastic sleeves.

"How am I supposed to work with just four pictures in my book?" I ask.

She ignores me and hands me a list of eleven go-sees, which seems like a lot for the first day. Scarlett has three. I try to hide my confusion. "Go to the bookstore and get a *Plan de Paris*. It's a map that will be your bible with all the streets of Paris. If you need to use the ladies', use the café toilets."

"Do we have to buy something before we use their bathroom? They won't get mad?" I ask.

"No. Oh, and tips are included. You can stay all day in a café, if you want. Good luck." She picks up the phone and gives us her backside.

I'm so distracted and confused by the scene in the agency—Gerald, all Mr. Handsome and Charming, and Pepper, all cocky and aloof ripping my portfolio apart—that I slide on a pile of dog shit on the way to the bookstore. Parisians don't pick up dog shit. If my book is so bad, why did they even want me to come?

We find the bookstore and the little maroon *Plan de Paris*. The cashier growls angry words in French while I write a traveler's check. I can see he wants cash but I haven't gotten any yet. The *Plan de Paris* is similar to the *Thomas Guide* map I use at home, but in French.

"Good luck today, Scarlett." I hug her.

"Same to you." We roll our eyes at each other like, yeah right. She heads off for face and hair appointments and I take off for fashion go-sees.

I descend tentatively into the Metro, which is now a hive of activity compared to last night's silence. Everyone rushes around, staring straight ahead. No one says hello or smiles at one another like in California. It's all strictly business.

I wander around reading my map trying to figure out which platform I should be on. Finally, I find it and stand in the crowd holding my white portfolio. As the Metro speeds in and screeches to a halt, chaos ensues. An ear-crushing buzz fills the tunnel until somebody flips the latch that opens the doors. Everybody pushes and shoves into the cars without a single "excuse me," then the capsule of putrid smells takes off like a rocket.

On the first sharp turn, I slam into an oily-looking man. I apologize in English and grab a pole.

My Paris Planning composite

THE MOUTH OF TRUTH

Photo studios in Los Angeles are notoriously hard to find. Photographers don't want thieves stealing their expensive equipment, so they're hidden behind plain, nondescript walls. Paris takes this art of disguise to a new level.

But first I need to find the right platform and the right station to get off and transfer trains a few times, find the exit, and walk in the correct direction block after block, looking for the right street, address, door, and person—without speaking French, because Parisians in 1980 refuse to speak English. I am shockingly on time for my 10 A.M. go-see with *Elle* magazine in an old stone mansion.

The receptionist escorts me to a cavernous white room with rolling racks of clothes. Shoes and accessories are piled on the floor. A petite woman, probably in her thirties, walks in, scowling, looking at her watch. I still don't know that it's rude to be on time in Paris. On time in Paris is fifteen minutes late. She hands me a dress. I don't see a dressing room, so I change right there while she flips through my now small selection of photos.

In Los Angeles, I was used to clients liking me so even though I was nervous, I felt upbeat. The reality hits me that if this one lady likes me, I can shoot for *Elle* and take those gorgeous shots straight to New York and make it big. But that's not what happens.

She looks at my book, then back at me, shakes her head no, lights a cigarette, motions for me to do a spin. I spin around and she shakes her head no again, saying, *"Non, ce n'est pas bien. Merci, au revoir."* I am dismissed. Not even a Polaroid. As she leaves the room, I wonder if there is any chance she could change her mind. Maybe she'll call the agency and actually hire me. Maybe. Not.

I'm intensely focused on finding my way to my next go-see with no idea where I'm going. Plus, I have ten more appointments in this maze of a city. I'm walking down the street, distracted, when suddenly a filthy dreadlocked man jumps out from a doorway and shoves a bloody, wiggling rat right in my face. I scream, and he breaks into a diabolical laugh. What kind of asshole does this? I run away while he chases me for a block with the bloody rat.

I make it to the next go-see in a studio with about fifty other girls. They're all American, Canadian, and European. They are never Asian, African, Indian, or Latin. I wait for two hours to be seen. Three women and one man, obviously the photographer, flip through my book, pointing at the photos. They look up at me and speak French to one another. I wish I could understand them. It doesn't sound good. I imagine the worst. They hand me my book with a *"Merci, au revoir."*

About noon, I duck inside a café to eat and pee, where the thick, moist air reeks of wet dog, cigarettes, stale liquor, and old piss. Eventually, I crave rancid café odors, but not today. I pull out my *French for Travelers* book and say to the waiter, *"Café seevoos plate."* He walks away, waving his hands in the air. He's not putting up with me.

I ask the man behind the bar where the restroom is. He points to the stairs. I descend to find a tiny closet with a square porcelain floor. There are nonslip places for my feet on either side of a hole. I pull my jeans down and squat over the hole. No toilet paper. I drip-dry and leave hungry.

I continue dragging myself around from go-see to go-see, each more depressing than the previous one. I don't receive a shred of approval, not even a smile. All I get are rude, cold people pointing at my flaws and whispering about me in French.

After a day full of confusion and rejection, I climb the stairs out of the Metro at dusk. I'm lost, hungry, tired, and broken. I take a shaky breath in and as I exhale, I break down crying. Paris doesn't want me. What the fuck was I thinking? This place is hell!

I stand on the corner as darkness falls around me, crying intensely but silently. I can hold in the sound of my sadness but can't control my pouring tears, fast breathing, or pounding head. I've never felt like such a loser in my life, except maybe back in sixth grade when the entire class dumped their bins of trash on my head on trash pickup day. Everybody is against me. I'm a freak. I'm not what they want. I'm ugly, dirty, and flawed. Not pretty, fresh, and loved.

But what can I do? If I give up and go back to Los Angeles, I still can't make enough money to live well on. I've got to make it. I can't give up. I've got to get the pictures and go to New York. If I make it big in New York, I'll have enough money to be independent and free. I'm not giving up on my goal. But what if I don't make it? Then what will I do?

I skip the last two appointments and flag a taxi to the hotel, crying the whole way.

When I enter the hotel lobby, I stand and look around. I notice how dirty and derelict everything is, from the peeling wallpaper to the cracked floor tiles. The manager pops up from under his desk, startling me. He points to himself, smiling and saying, "Jean Paul." His salt-and-pepper-colored frizzy hair is poking out in every direction, like a bird's nest. His wrinkly clothes are four sizes too big and his trousers, rolled at the ankle, must have belonged to someone else. He obviously dresses from the lost-and-found bin.

"I'm Jill." I point to myself and try to stop sobbing. He comes round the desk and kisses me on both cheeks with his greasy, unshaven, prickly face, which feels surprisingly comforting and makes me cry even more.

He catches me looking at the long, thin needles that protrude from his forehead and his ears. He arranges his hair, trying to hide them, saying, *"Je souffre de migraines. C'est l'acupuncture,"* and hands me my skeleton key with the dirty, wine-colored tassel attached.

"Thanks." I turn to the stairs and take a deep breath. As I ascend the four flights, I fantasize about a hot bath. If this hotel doesn't have heat, it's got to have hot water, right? I grab the pressed, white linen hand towel from my room and go down the hall to the *salle de bains*.

I step in the tub and turn on the hot water but, even after a long time, it's still freezing cold. I wash the essentials and dry off with the tiny towel. I run, freezing, back to my room and jump under the covers. I made it through the first day. Barely.

✦

I roll out of bed and pee in the bidet. Fuck that freezing hallway. It's Saturday—my face and my ass belong to me today.

I grab my cold Levi's from the floor. My knees ache from the pounding they endured all week. Walking on granite sidewalks all day in heels, or even flats, made my knees swell and now they're so tight I can hardly bend them. Years later, I learn that I've got a genetic connective tissue disease called Ehlers-Danlos syndrome. I pop the water blisters on my feet with a safety pin and throw on my tennis shoes.

Breakfast is in the basement, through the rough-hewn limestone arch. I duck under, but Scarlett sails right through. We sit down at one of the small tables among the other foreign guests. I try to imagine the thousands of souls who must have eaten here and it makes me feel safe somehow.

Jean Paul walks in with a big smile and brings us cafés au lait, warm baguettes, and triangles of soft cheese. I slather the warm bread with butter and apricot jam and dig in. Never have I ever tasted bread this delicious in my life. I eat the entire six-inch chunk. The French baguette would soon become a huge source of stress, since it's always available, cheap, and so damn good.

Scarlett says, "I'm not eating all this. I'll eat half. No butter and jam." Then she sets her cheese in the middle of the table.

"Can I have your cheese?" I ask.

Tourists at the other table give us the stink eye knowing we're responsible for blowing out the hotel electrical panel. An American blow dryer was too much to handle.

I bundle up in my ridiculous-looking, long, purple goose-down jacket, while Scarlett piles on layers of mountain-girl clothes. My face is numb with the cold as we stroll along streets, so quiet compared to the hustle of the workweek. With no destination in mind, we wind up at the Luxembourg Gardens. It's so nice to just walk and talk—no go-sees, no one to impress.

"How long were you in LA?" I ask.

"Only two months."

"So, you came to model? I guess they don't have much modeling work in Portland, do they?"

"No, they don't," she says, laughing, "but I actually came to LA for cosmetology school."

"You did?"

"Yeah, I was studying to be a makeup artist when someone from the school told me I should do face and hair modeling. So I interviewed at Wilhelmina and they signed me."

"That's amazing! So, do you really love doing makeup?"

"I do! I'm gonna do it again when I'm done modeling."

"Would you do my makeup, sometime?"

"Of course!" She smiles.

I pepper her with questions all around the gardens until we stop in front of the marble statue called *La Bocca della Verità*—The Mouth of Truth. Legend says that if you tell a lie with your hand in her mouth, she'll bite it off. The statue is so playful and beautiful.

I've never seen nude art like this. There's no sexy vibe like in my dad's collection of lusty nudes hanging in the garage and our den. This graceful nude woman doesn't make me feel uncomfortable; she makes me feel good. I want to be like her, appreciated for her playful, womanly spirit, not just her beauty and sexuality.

We wander through an open-air farmers' market with bright orange carrots and ruby red beets, so fresh they have dirt still clinging to them. Onions, potatoes, and leeks overflow from wood crates. I don't know what a *fromagerie* is, but small mountains of tiny cheeses are artfully arranged and piled high in every shade of yellow, cream, and orange imaginable. The vendors beam with pride over their products. It is nothing like the supermarkets back home.

"Bonjour mademoiselles!" the butchers shout as we pass the meat stall, wearing aprons stained with blood. Huge hunks of meat hang overhead. We giggle at the reconstructed ducks that have been cleaned and reunited with their feathers and orange bills for display.

The currency is a mystery, so as I pay for my goods, I show the vendor my bills and coins. They take the proper amount and count back to me, generously teaching me how to use French money. Soon, I've got bags of fresh yogurt, cheese, fruit, bread, and a dusty, homemade bottle of one-franc wine.

Scarlett and I stroll slowly back to the hotel. I tie my bag of yogurt and cheese outside the window, on the balcony railing, hoping the pigeons don't steal it. Who needs a refrigerator in this weather?

Later that night, we slice the cheese with my Swiss Army knife and devour it with bread and wine. With no television or music, we find other ways to entertain ourselves, things that would never happen back home.

We tear pages from my journal and make a backgammon board. Aspirin tablets and coins are our playing pieces. We play for hours, taking turns pulling hand-numbered scraps, like dice, from an empty yogurt container. I look at Scarlett's sweet face and feel deep gratitude that she is here with me. As we play, I kind of pull away to watch our scene. . . .

I'm in my favorite brown-and-white men's flannel pajamas, a wool sweater, and three layers of socks. Scarlett is just as bundled up in her bright red coat and ski cap. Even with the struggles and difficulties, I feel something totally new. There's not a single soul around watching me, telling me what to do. There are no house rules. I can do what I want, when I want, and no one knows or cares. No peer pressure, no parent pressure, and even no friend pressure. I'm completely unknown, anonymous. A brand-new sense of freedom fills my entire being as I watch myself laugh, feeling totally safe and at peace. I'm doing exactly what I want in this moment. I am free.

Bread and wine, aspirin and coin backgammon,
Paris, winter 1980

ADJUSTMENTS

As one challenging day of interviews bleeds into the next, I feel like my body is held hostage in Paris, with my mind detached and stuck in LA. I'm frustrated and lonely and miss everything about America. Paris is a bigger adjustment than I could have imagined. Mostly it's the simple things I miss, like soft toilet paper or menus I can read.

Los Angeles is always hot, but in Paris the gutters are frozen and sealed with ice crystals. And the rain! I've never seen so much rain. The sky is dark and covered in a blanket of gray clouds. It's shocking, coming from the sunny blue skies of California, and pretty depressing too.

I'm used to speeding all over in my red sports car, from the beach to the city, out to clubs and restaurants, and over to friends' houses. Here, I have to walk and take the Metro, which never winds up being close to where I'm going anyway, so I still have to walk. Back home, I always know where I am but here I'm always lost and confused.

In Los Angeles, I lived on healthy salad bars and tasty Mexican food. Here, I eat bread, cheese, and wine and always feel bloated. The French bistros don't offer healthy salads, just fatty German sausages, baguette sandwiches, and premade croque monsieurs—bread stuffed with fatty cheese, butter, and ham. I feel fat but can't go to the gym. They don't have gyms here. None that I can find anyway. I'm used to working out three times a week, plus swimming. I feel my muscles fading away, except in my legs from all the walking. I wish I could afford a car, but I don't know where I'm going and can't speak French, so how could I read the road signs, pass a driving test, or buy a car?

At home, I fit in. Here I stand out like a freak. I don't know how to dress, I can't speak the language, and I can't figure out the modeling market. It's nothing like Los Angeles.

Even though I run around on go-sees all week, I'm not used to having this much free time. Normally, I'm busy with my friends in between work. I don't know what to do with all my nervous energy, but I've got to get it out, so I start writing at cafés—a lot. I sit between interviews, writing letters home or in my journal. Sometimes I sit and stare and watch the people trudging by. I've never written this much or sat in silence for so long in my life!

Even though I broke up with Jack before leaving the US, I miss the sex. It's not easy for me to have sex. Jack was the first boy I ever slept with. Sex and I have a complicated relationship. I fear it and crave it at the same time.

I miss my friends, I miss the sun, I miss my car, and I hate these hotels. I miss speaking English so badly that I go to the American Legion in Paris to talk with old war veterans.

My favorite reminder of home that I've found so far is a restaurant called Jo Allen, because everything is in English. The waiters even speak broken English, although with thick French accents. I always get the same thing: carrot ginger soup and afterward, a warm brownie topped with a mountain of whipped cream. I eat slowly and enjoy being somewhere that feels a little more like home.

Misery in Paris, winter 1980

PARIS PHOTOS

My first shoot is for *Paris Match*, which I assume is a fashion magazine, but later learn is closer to *Newsweek*. Pin-Up studio on Avenue Jean-Moulin isn't easy to find in the pouring rain. I've been using my white vinyl portfolio to shield me from the downpour instead of buying an umbrella.

Inside, Pink Floyd's *The Wall* is blasting and stylists buzz around. The smell of cigarettes and espresso hangs in the air. The studio is cavernous, with tall ceilings and white walls. No faded wallpaper or antique woodwork here.

The photographer yells to me, "*Bonjour! Commencez les cheveux et le maquillage, s'il vous plaît,*" and returns to his lighting setup.

"*Bonjour,*" I say, and head to the makeup room, with walls of mirrors and clear, round bulbs, and take a seat among the other models. The hairstylist puts my hair in hot rollers, while the makeup artist jumps in, chatting away in French. He dabs concealer under my eyes, covers my face in foundation, brushes on blush, then eye shadow, eyeliner, and mascara. With steady hands, he lines my lips and fills them with lipstick and gloss. After the hairstylist runs his hands through my hair, I'm ready to shoot.

The photographer indicates for me to pull my V-necked T-shirt down off my shoulders to just above my breasts, which always means a face shot. No gorgeous clothes today.

Being comfortable with nudity comes bit by tiny bit. For me, it began with growing up in the heat waves of Los Angeles, where I ran around in my bikini. Then, when I worked as a swim instructor, a bikini was my uniform. Working as a fit model for a swimwear company, my breasts and ass were tools—shaping devices that perfectly fitting swimsuits were formed upon. I've learned to separate my body from my inner self. I see my body as a tool with many uses, from creating good-fitting swimsuits to promoting products. I use my body to make money, selling everything from swimwear and sportswear to soap and soda. It is confusing sometimes though, because there are times when I need to detach, like for work or if men are staring at me, and there are other times when I need to feel connected with my body in order to feel peace and rest. I constantly go in and out of connecting with myself.

On location shoots in California we change clothes in public— on the beach under a towel or in cars. At fashion shows, male and female models, makeup artists, stylists, and designers all work backstage while I stand in my tiny, nude thong, no bra, because you can't distract from the clothes with undergarments poking about. Nudity becomes no big deal at work, which is a very different situation from my crazy mixed-up feelings about sex. Anyway, we're just all there to do our jobs.

I'm led to a large circular arrangement of shoes on the floor. I tiptoe on the pristine white studio paper, careful not to leave a footprint, and get into position with my head in the center of the shoes on the floor, as directed.

The French stylist has wild red hair, thick black eyeliner, and red lips. She wears Levi's 501s and a pink sweatshirt belted tight at her waist. She crawls on her hands and knees, arranging shoes around my head like peacock plumes. The concrete floor under the paper feels like a block of ice against my entire backside. The photographer's assistant holds the light meter over my face with a pop. He reports the numbers to the photographer, who hangs over me on a ladder, shooting test Polaroids.

Once he's happy, he switches to his 35mm camera and starts clicking away. *"Bien, bon travail. Regardez-moi."* The lights pop loudly each time, setting off the flash.

I ignore the cold floor and my head surrounded by shoes. I pretend that I'm looking at my best friend or someone I love as I stare directly into the glass camera lens. Since the camera picks up all my emotions, I focus hard on peaceful thoughts. Whenever I smile, the photographer keeps yelling, *"Ferme ta bouche!"* (Close your mouth!) It took me a while to learn that in Paris I wasn't supposed to smile for the camera like they wanted me to in Hollywood.

No one teaches you how to be a model. I had to figure it out myself. Every shoot is an opportunity to learn the lighting and angles that complement or sabotage my face, my body, and the clothes I'm trying to sell. Every job has a new set of personalities, tools, and challenges to learn from.

Every model has their go-to pose and facial expression. Just like Ben Stiller with his "Blue Steel" look in *Zoolander*, we all have an angle we know works every time. We learn how to position our face on the exact right plane opposite the camera lens. It makes each feature of our face look exactly how we want it to. You want bigger lips? Push them toward the camera. Slimmer hips? Twist them sideways. Twisting your body around the right way makes all the difference and is definitely a required skill!

My next job is for a laundry detergent, where I am dressed up in a sweet, pink button-front blouse to look like a French housewife. I snub my nose at the pile of dirty laundry in one shot, and joyfully hold their product in the next. Product photographers are easy to work with because they are more focused on their perfect lighting than on my flaws.

Next, I shoot nursing bras, holding a cute baby. I'm a little young to be a nursing mother, but as long as they pay me, I don't care. Of course, none of these jobs will be going into my book. They wouldn't impress New York fashion editors or photographers in the least.

I am finally sent to Dior for a runway show go-see. The neighborhood is so clean compared to mine, which bustled with working-class people, immigrants, and tourists. Chic apartments line both sides of Avenue Montaigne. Older people wearing expensive-looking clothes dine at bistros with polished brass railings. These restaurants are on a whole different level than the ones I've been going to.

A uniformed guard opens the door at 30 Avenue Montaigne, where an older woman in a white lab coat escorts me through the boutique and up a curved white marble staircase into the atelier.

I had never seen an actual Christian Dior piece in person, only in magazines. There are so many beautiful things I would have loved to touch and to try on, but wouldn't have dared ask. Regardless, couture is for wealthy, older ladies, not struggling models. The walls of the design room are covered in fashion illustrations signed by Marc Bohan, Dior's designer. I know his name from years of studying *Vogue*.

Four other models show up and all of us are unusually quiet. Dior felt serious, like church.

The stylists flip through our books, whisper to one another in French, and then hand us dresses to put on. As we come out of the changing rooms, they gesture for us to walk across the room for them, which is when I panic because I don't know the European runway walk. I walked so many shows in Los Angeles, but this is Paris Haute Couture—a totally different caliber of show and style.

One of the girls, a pageant girl, Miss Missouri or something, confidently goes first in her pageant-style walk, which looks ridiculous in the Dior atelier. I dive right in after her, walking with even less grace than the pageant model. Then, the third girl walks forward as if she's floating, blank-faced and elegant, proving to Miss Missouri and me how far off the mark we are. I know I blew it. I wish someone would teach me how to do the French walk. I'm so mad at myself for blowing Dior! But how could I possibly know how to do the walk without being shown? I feel trapped in a cage.

♦

After running around for weeks, I finally land an actual cover shoot for *Girls* magazine. Since it is the French equivalent to *Teen* in America, I assume it will be high quality. I knock at the door of the studio and am welcomed inside by the photographer, but the studio isn't much bigger than a bedroom. Dusty props and lighting equipment are strewn about carelessly and junk covers the floor. It isn't compulsively organized like every other photographer's studio I have been in.

No makeup room, makeup artist, or hairstylist, and no fashion stylist either. I do my own hair and makeup, and the photographer actually irons the clothes himself. My hopes for a great cover dissolve in an instant.

Every single shred of excitement and hope to make great photographic fashion art in Paris is being met with defeat. I didn't know how different Paris would be. One thing's for sure, I'm not the girl Paris wants.

How could I know, at such a young age, that sometimes the reasons we do things are not for the reasons we think? It never dawned on me that the reason I came to Paris could be anything different than making it as a successful model. How could I possibly imagine the unexpected results of my choices and decisions?

I had no plan to fall in love with Paris, or anybody else for that matter. I didn't have an agenda for finding inner peace. I came here to have a career, and that means I am here for one reason only— those damn elusive pictures. I was never looking for fame. That wasn't my goal. I wanted freedom, independence, and a feeling of accomplishment—like I had arrived at my destination, totally satisfied. I wanted a steady source of income that would give me the resources to live how I wanted, with no one telling me what to do! I figured that if I could achieve this with a job I loved, creating photographic art with the best of the best designers, photographers, makeup artists, and stylists, I'd be happy for sure!

It's clear I need to study the market because whatever I'm doing is totally not working. I go to a newsstand and purchase every important fashion magazine and sit in a café, drinking my café au lait with two cubes of sugar, studying the editorial pages. Every single model has long straight hair, narrow hips, and bright white teeth. My hair is barely to my shoulders, and even though I'm so thin, my hipbones are wider than the girls' in the pages. There is nothing I can do about my hipbones, but I really should have had my teeth capped like my Hollywood agent recommended. I wish my hair would hurry up and grow.

At the same time I'm feeling all this angst and frustration, I am totally unaware that I'm slowly falling in love with this city. Over time, Paris will root deep down into my soul and become part of me.

Paris café, 1980

JULIE ON THE COUCH

"You and Scarlett have been invited to a special party tonight. Wear a dress and be there at nine," Pepper says, handing me my list of go-sees.

All day long, images run through my mind of how amazing the party will be. Just like the party pictures in the back of *Vogue Paris*— rock stars, artists, designers, world-famous photographers, they'll all be there! At least I've got this to distract me from the reality of trudging all over this dirty city.

That evening, Scarlett was taking way too long to get ready. It was my mom all over again—the eternal primping. "Come on, Scarlett, let's go, we're gonna be late. Pepper said to be there at nine."

"I'm doing my eyes." She's sitting on the bed, leaning into her compact and stroking her lashes with mascara.

"Okay, now?" I pace.

"I need to finish my eye shadow, and still do my hair."

"It doesn't need to be perfect. Can't we just go? You look great!" Nothing I say makes her go faster. I've got to wait it out. Scarlett has her own style—I guess it's because she's from the Pacific Northwest that she hides her beautiful body under baggy, nature-lover clothes. Plaid flannel shirts and hiking pants are the total opposite of her superfeminine face and hair. She's definitely got the more practical shoes though. My ankle-strap black suede heels are a nightmare, and my clothes aren't working either, by the way. All I've got are T-shirts, a pair of unflattering jeans, two skirts, two sweaters, and my digital Star Wars watch.

We find the address Pepper gave us, and it's a mansion hidden behind tall gray stone walls. We buzz the intercom and a butler opens the gate, holding a platter of champagne glasses. He leads us in and takes our coats. Instantly, I could tell this was not the party I had hoped for. It is totally quiet and there are no young people from the fashion business—just old businessmen. Two of them come over and greet us in French, to which I respond, "Oh, sorry, I don't speak French." Then say to Scarlett, "Let's go watch the fire," and walk away toward the fireplace.

I stand with my back to the fire, scanning the room. I don't get it. Clusters of businessmen stand around talking and drinking. Most are in suits, yet others are wearing Arab robes with headscarves. It looks like they've just finished their political negotiations or something.

I notice a young woman lying on the couch. I can tell she modeled in the past, because of her extreme beauty, but now she's a little older and more voluptuous. She looks at us as if through a thick fog. "Hey, girls . . ."

We walk over, and Scarlett stands while I sit on the corner of the couch by her feet. "Hi, I'm Jill and this is Scarlett."

She raises her head a little saying, "You're new here, aren't you?"

"New? You mean in Paris?" I ask. Her head dips up and down like she is going to pass out. She lies back on a black velvet pillow. "I'm Julie. I live here."

"How long have you lived here?" I ask.

"Eight years." Then, with a slurring whisper, she says, "Don't do it. You'll get stuck." Scarlett and I look at each other. Julie cocks her head, rolling her eyes toward the men behind us.

She reminds me of the "lost girls" of Hollywood: the group of models I tried to avoid getting pulled into. Some of them hung out at the Playboy Mansion, testing their fate. Would they meet a wealthy actor and live happily ever after? Or were they on a fast track to a rich old man's bed and drug addiction? Some started out as high-priced hookers who eventually wound up addicted to heroin. They'd get stuck with these men because they needed their drugs, then when they lost their fresh healthy looks, they'd be sold to other men for sex. If the routine in Paris is anything like Los Angeles, a man would use her for a while then share her with his friends. Shoot her up and fuck her. Girls were kept like house pets. I wasn't going to let that happen to me before, and I certainly wasn't willing to go down that road now in Paris.

"Mademoiselles, come see the football game—France is ahead!" Our host tried to distract us from Julie.

Luckily, Scarlett whispers in my ear, "Let's get outta here." We bluff, asking where the toilet is, and bolt for the door. We run through the garden, out the gate, and onto the street. Adrenaline runs through my body, while images of Julie and that room full of men race through my mind. We run like we're escaping danger. I'm confused why Pepper would send us there. At best, those men may have owned big magazines, and at worst, they wanted to have sex with us.

The next morning, along with my go-see list, Pepper hands me a note with the time and address for another party. I'm not so sure I want to go. Maybe this one will be different. I never tell her what happened at the last one.

Scarlett and I are greeted at the door of another gorgeous mansion, where a handsome male model in a black leather jacket and jeans welcomes us and pours us each a glass of red wine. Now this is better, I think. Old-time French jazz and candlelight fill the huge room with vaulted ceilings. Dark wood tables and blue velvet couches are accessorized with a bohemian mash-up of textiles and pillows.

Outside, in the back courtyard, an animated game of horseshoes is in full swing, with guests laughing and taunting one another competitively. Gorgeous models mix with obvious fashion insiders. People in fashion are easy to spot by the way they dress and act. If you're in the industry yourself, you can pick one out a block away.

A god of a man introduces himself to me, asking if I am American in his super-low voice and French accent, "*Êtes-vous américain, chérie? Je suis Jean Marie.*" He leans in and kisses my cheeks slowly and softly—not the usual fast kiss-kiss. I'm totally caught off guard and actually feel my vagina pulse.

He's probably the most handsome man I've ever seen in person. He's super tall and muscular with brown hair, brown eyes, and a wicked smile. I have an unexpected rush of lust and am actually afraid of what I might do. If we wind up kissing tonight, it is definitely not going to stop there. I feel him turn that inner locked key to my sexuality, and it scares me. Sex with me is all or nothing, and I've only ever slept with one man, Jack. I'm terrified and excited at the same time. I'm always afraid of losing control over my body's sexual urges and I try to keep a lid on it. All this insane conflict is a result of growing up the way I did, but I don't know it yet. Turns out, Jean Marie is a male model and member of the French Olympic rowing team. No wonder he looks like that. We're ushered into the dining room, diverting our lust. I take a breath in relief.

The hostess stands on top of one of the many long tables lined up in the dining hall, banging a wooden spoon on a copper frying pan, yelling, "*Bienvenue! Bon appétit!*" In the center of each table are huge-ass bowls of spaghetti and red sauce—simple and glamorous at once. I sit between Scarlett and an innocent-looking young French guy named Henri. We all chat clumsily through the language barrier.

After dinner, everyone mingles as the music changes from old-timey to French pop. I hear rumblings about going to a club. Scarlett joins another group while I head out with Henri. I'm pretty tipsy from the wine and smile at him and say, "I'll only go with you if I can drive your car."

"*Oui, bien sûr!*" he says enthusiastically. "*Allons-y!*" ("Let's go!")

Henri has a tiny red Renault Le Car with a manual transmission, but the gear stick isn't on the floor—it juts out of the dashboard. I have absolutely no idea how to drive it. My instincts take over and I figure it out as I go, speeding around the roundabout at the Arc de Triomphe and down the Champs Élysées.

"*À droite! À droite!*" Henri screams, pointing right, and "*À gauche! À gauche!*" pointing left. I make a mental note to add these to my collection of French words. I have no idea where I parked the car.

European discos are totally different from American nightclubs. Small, round cocktail tables are set low to the ground, surrounded by purple velvet poufs to sit on. Instead of rock or new wave, electronica pulses and colored lights flash onto the crowd on the dance floor. My group is VIP with their own lockers of booze behind the bar. Bottles of liquor are delivered and set up with buckets of ice and mixers. Girls are dancing with girls, and I recognize some of them from French magazines and feel pangs of jealousy. I remember one of them with her blond hair to her waist, while there I am with shoulder-length brown hair. I join in anyway, dancing for hours, until I remember my early job call.

"Scarlett, I'm going home!" I yell, waving, trying to get her attention.

Henri jumps up. "*Chérie*, I will drive you!" I am so relieved that I don't have to figure out how to get home. Ice has formed on the outside of the car window and the heater fogs the windshield but feels good on my feet. I kick off my shoes, relax, and take in the view as he drives.

Cafés look so pretty at night, their chairs stacked upside down on top of the tables. Colored lights reflect on the wet road from street signs above. I lose myself in the beauty. Henri puts his hand on the back of my neck. I think he is going to pet me, but he grabs a fistful of hair and shoves my face in his crotch. His pants are un-zipped and he's aroused. I struggle to pull away, but he shoves my face down hard on his penis all the way to my hotel.

The second he stops the car, I fly out, run to the door, and wildly press the buzzer. I can feel him coming up behind me. The night clerk opens the door, and I hurry past, yelling, "No, please don't let him in!" Of course, he doesn't understand. Henri chases me up the stairs, pushes his way into my room, and shoves me onto the bed. He rips my blouse open so hard and fast that buttons bounce around the room.

"No! Please no!" I yell.

He jams his hand under my skirt, pulling on my underwear, and I kick him hard in the stomach and he flies against the wall. He quickly gathers himself and leaves. I lock the door behind him and collapse on the bed. I lie struggling with the reality that I was almost raped. I turn out the light and try to calm the hell down. When I imagine in detail what could have happened, I can't take it. I try to pry my brain off the terrifying images racing through my mind. I try desperately to detach.

About an hour later, Scarlett comes in, panting. "You won't be-lieve what that creep Henri did to me! He attacked me in his car the whole way home! I almost jumped out while it was moving. That guy's a pervert!"

"I went through the same thing! He followed me in here! I kicked him really hard and he finally left."

"What's wrong with these people? I'm not going to any more of Pepper's parties," Scarlett says.

"Me either."

We barely sleep. I wake to the sound of rain pattering softly on the wood shutters and pull the covers over my head. All I can see are scary flashbacks. I feel him grabbing the back of my head and shoving it down. I can't stop the visions, so I get up.

We're so exhausted that we barely speak over breakfast. I want to talk to Gerald or Pepper about the party, but I don't know what I expect them to say. Plus, I'm not very good at standing up for myself. That is a skill I never learned. I feel so insanely vulnerable and even blame myself for what happened. Why did I even get in his car?

It dawns on me how dependent I am on the agency. They're like a quasi-family I depend on for survival. I get jobs, money, guidance, and moral support from them because I don't know anybody in this country besides Scarlett, and she doesn't know anybody either!

The agency has the power to take me to the top or hold me down at the bottom of the pool to drown. I see new girls come into town and watch as Gerald sends them straight over to shoot for *Vogue* without even an interview. He's the most powerful agent, not just in France, but in all of Europe. Magazines and photographers ask him which models they should use. I wish he'd tell them to use me.

Pepper looks up as I walk straight toward her. "Can we talk a minute?" I ask.

"*Bien sûr*, sweet thing, but before I forget, Jill, you landed the La Redoute campaign. That's good news, *chérie*. You shoot next week." I stand, fuming internally with a blank look on my face. "What's the matter, aren't you excited?"

I can't tell her how I really feel, so I start with "I can't go to any more parties." I wait for a response. She stares at me with big eyes, not moving. Gerald overhears and marches over.

"What's this, Gilles? You have a problem with my parties?" He is pissed off.

My face flushes hot. "I don't feel comfortable. . . ."

"Oh, you're not comfortable? Okay. No parties, no interviews!" He throws his hands in the air and storms back to his desk. He turns the music up super loud, lights a smoke, and picks up his phone.

"Sorry, Jill," Pepper says. I'm shaking inside. I take a deep breath. I know if I don't like the way things work over here, there are hundreds of models who would love to take my place.

Later that day, I call the agency from the pay phone to check in, just like every evening. Pepper answers, sounding distracted. "Hey, no appointments for tomorrow. And listen, you and Scarlett are going back to working only with me. Gerald won't be booking you anymore."

His message is clear.

"Alright, talk to you later," I say, defeated. She'd already hung up.

Wearing Dad's fireman clothes, Downey, California, 1965

POLLYWOGS

1960s, California

Downey, California, is my hometown. It's just ten miles southeast of downtown Los Angeles, surrounded by the 5, 710, 605, and 91 freeways. Downey is hot, flat, and still.

I'm specifically from South Downey, which is a different world from nicer, safer, and richer North Downey. My block is close to an area called Dogpatch, named after the gang. Paramount and Compton are close by. My dad is a fireman in Watts, a fifteen-minute drive. In our neighborhood, gang fights, drug deals, and home robberies are daily occurrences.

In addition to the sketchy area and violence just outside my home, violence is inside too. My parents married at only twenty and twenty-one, and had my sister right away, and me three years later. They both dragged their toxic upbringings with them. My dad's dad was a violent alcoholic who beat my dad with his fists, and his mother wasn't exactly warm and fuzzy. My mom couldn't stand to be around her own mother, but she loved her dad. Her mom had a wicked temper and could throw an angry tantrum. She always felt that her mother favored her little brother over her.

Although my dad isn't quite as violent with us as his dad was, he is frightening and can switch from laughing to hitting in a split second. I never know when it's coming. He can freak out over just about anything. I tiptoe through my childhood, trying to avoid his wrath.

✦

When I'm five or six my favorite thing to do is walk past my neighborhood block over to Long's Dairy. I climb up onto the painted whitewood fences and yell "Mooooo" at the cows, trying to get them to moo back. I gather a handful of hay from under the fence and climb up to feed the cows. I'm always on the lookout for a pregnant one, hoping to watch her give birth. The calf comes out in a big, gooey clear sac that the mother licks until the baby is clean and tries to stand up. I love watching the baby nurse, and it is my dream to milk a cow someday. If I have some spare coins with me, I go to the front of the drive-through dairy and buy an ice cream sandwich.

Tahitian Village is a motel behind our block. I hop the neighbors' block wall fence or walk around to the end of the block to Rosecrans Avenue and turn left where a big wooden bridge arches over a lagoon. There are tiki torches and an old ship's hull with a huge carved mermaid. I walk over the bridge, through the gift shop, and into the open atrium in the middle of two stories of rooms with orange doors.

There is a tropical garden with palms and ferns and a miniature, algae-filled, fake stream in the center. I am on the hunt for pollywogs. Tiny pollywogs, pollywogs halfway turned into baby frogs with legs, tiny frogs, and full-grown toads all wiggled and jumped around. Sometimes motel guests had squished some of them on the walkway. It's survival of the fittest. I grab a few pollywogs and baby frogs and put them in my pocket, or in a Tupperware container with algae water, and rush home. I put everything in a glass bowl with some tap water and place it under the elephant ferns in our front-yard planter. Then I go fly-catching. I grab the fly swatter from the kitchen and smash flies on our garbage cans and put them in with the pollywogs and baby frogs.

Most of them die. But, some grow into full-grown frogs, jumping around in our planter until they hop out, wander into the street, and get flattened by cars.

I relate to the pollywogs. Those half-formed frogs. I'm just a half-formed girl, between a baby and an adult woman. I'm at the mercy of my caretakers, and just like the pollywogs, I'm not given the environment that I really need to thrive. I need to be nurtured and free to develop and grow in a nontoxic ecosystem. Yet, I'm just as guilty. I take the pollywogs from their homes and feed them dead flies. I try to nurture them but do a very poor job.

✦

Dinnertime is a nightmare. I survey and check for broccoli or asparagus. Choosing to not eat things I hate is never an option. Washing it down with milk isn't either. Since I'm still small, the table comes up to my chin. I don't like sitting on stacks of Yellow Pages anymore.

I stare at my plate nervously. If I don't eat fast, Dad will set the timer. My big sister eats in silence, staying under the radar. Mom tinkers at the sink and doesn't come to the table until we're done.

Dad sets the avocado-green kitchen timer and puts it in front of my plate. Five minutes. I sit frozen, watching it tick, and try to get the courage to swallow the damn broccoli. *Ding!* "Dammit, Jill!" He yanks me out of my chair by my elbow and shoves me onto my bed in my dark bedroom.

"Pull down your pants!" I obey and sit on the edge of the bed. He slaps me hard on each bony thigh. First they sting, then they burn like fire. I close my eyes terrified, trying not to fall apart, and the pain in my soul hurts more than the throbbing waves of pain in my legs.

"Go eat your goddamn broccoli!" Red hand-shaped welts rise. Sometimes they're bruised in the morning. I hold my breath as long as I can, crying silently, so he won't hit me for crying. Crying makes him even madder. I control my breathing, taking small, shallow puffs of air so he won't notice I'm sobbing. I'm broken. My face drips wet with tears and snot.

I hurry to my plate and sit in a frightened, silent trance— hyperalert and detached. I try to eat the broccoli again as he resets the timer.

◆

Mom and Dad make so much noise in the bedroom groaning. We have no idea what's going on, but we don't like it. I put a glass to the door to listen. I still don't get it. I climb on my dresser and listen through the heating vent. It just sounds gross.

They're obsessed with sex and don't limit it to the bedroom. Mom walks around the house in a silky robe, naked underneath. She doesn't tie the tie because Dad will just untie it anyway. He can't help but grab at her nude body, suck her breasts, slap her ass, and tug her pussy hair. He does it at the dinner table often, where we are not under any circumstances allowed to leave. When I beg him to stop, he laughs like he's pleased at the reaction he's getting out of me. He puts Mom's ideas down with the basic message that she's stupid.

Right after, he'll say, "Girls, isn't your mom beautiful? Look at her boobs, they're perfect."

Women are for sex, not their minds or souls. Women are loved for their beauty and for giving men the sex they constantly crave. We answer, "Yes, she's pretty."

Dad loves pornography. Porno magazines are all over the house. *Penthouse* and *Oui* are in their bedroom, *Playboy* on the kitchen counter, and a stack of really raunchy ones under the sink in his bathroom. He reads *Playboy* while I eat breakfast with him. He leaves for the fire station so early and all I want to do is spend time with him. We discuss the centerfold girl's hobbies over toast and coffee.

Boxes of porno films are in the garage, but my parents don't know I know. Wall-to-wall nude centerfolds are stapled to the garage walls like wallpaper. Dad shares his detailed opinion about each woman's body parts with me. When his friends are in the garage, he talks about each woman on the walls like he knows them. Then he gives them his critique of the girls too.

At bedtime, I get in my bed and Dad comes and lies on top of me, trapping me. He grabs my bony wrists with his massive fist and throws them over my head, squeezing them so tight it feels like my bones are going to dislocate—a one-handed handcuff. With his other hand, he "tickles" me hard, digging his fingers between my ribs and jamming them into my armpits. While this is going on, he licks me wildly all over my neck, face, and deep into my ears with his hard, wet tongue until I burn with a hot rash from his beard. I lash side to side trying to scream—he covers my mouth. He laughs, enjoying the hell out of this.

When he finally leaves, I smell like saliva and aftershave, and am so nauseous I want to puke. I cry, but Mom never comes. I sneak into the bathroom to look into the mirror because my neck is on fire. My neck, cheeks, and ears are bright pink, with small red dots of blood breaking through the surface. I put a cold, wet washcloth on my neck to cool it down and wash with soap to get the putrid smell off. My childhood experiences instill a kind of terror and shame in me about sex. It will take me decades to recover.

◆

The fire station in Watts is like a second home to me. Since my dad's captain of the squad, he goes there even on days off. He checks on the guys, picks up his paycheck, does paperwork, and because he takes me everywhere with him, I go too. I love the fire station and am comfortable in a room full of firemen.

They let me climb on the truck, slide down the pole, and even punch the boxing bag in the gym. One day though when I'm in his office with him and another fireman, Dad says, "So, Jill's developing,

you know." Meaning my breasts. I panic and want to disappear. I had
no idea he knew, and why would he tell someone about it?

As a teen, when I start becoming a young woman, Dad stares at
my body and spews sarcastic, sexual comments and critiques of it.
It makes me feel self-conscious, like I'm always being watched. One
time, while we were on a waterskiing vacation at the Colorado River,
he starts talking about my body in front of the other teenage boys
and girls. I become so enraged that I take a swing at his face with my
fists. He's so big and strong, he easily catches them midair, proving
me powerless. He keeps this shit up on and off for years.

Years later, after another one of his lusty comments, I vividly
remember falling on my hands and knees, alone, on the fireplace
hearth and pounding the hard stone until my hands are swollen and
red. I writhe my whole body up and down while a soul-wrenching
howl escapes from deep within me. I scream out loud to God,
"Why didn't you give me a father I can trust? Why did you give me
a pervert?!"

I actually hear a voice inside me saying, *He's not your father, I
am.* That gives me something to think about. I write Dad a letter
saying that if he ever talks about my body again he will never see me
again—ever. He mellows out for a while, but I am on guard forever.

Mom is emotionally checked out. She doesn't show affection to
her two daughters like she does to her little dogs. She avoids us,
hiding in the bathroom or bedroom. I am positive she regrets giving
birth to us. I want to play with her jewelry, makeup, and clothes, but
I'm not allowed to touch them. When she leaves the house, I study
and touch all of her things, careful to put them back where they
were. I feel close to her through touching her stuff. I want her love
and affection so bad it hurts. I try not to bother her, but it's hard to
leave her alone. She has a wicked temper, but I'm not as afraid of
her as I am of Dad.

The only person welcome in our house is the Avon lady. I'm not
allowed to have friends over, which puts me in a weird spot, having

to explain why they can't come over to play, that I can only play at their houses. Eventually, Mom gets a job, I assume, to get away from my sister and me.

✦

When I was a little girl, my dad was my first hero. He was a fireman in probably the most dangerous station in the country. Battling the Watts riots in 1965, delivering babies, and bandaging stab and gunshot wounds was part of the job. In brushfire season, he'd be gone for weeks. When he'd return home, he would drop his soggy, ashy boots and turnout coat on the porch, and his helmet in the kitchen sink. He'd be limp with exhaustion and smell like a campfire.

Dad taught me to fix up cars and houses and sell them at a profit. I was his laborer in his house-painting business, and his swimming pool–cleaning job. We even worked cleaning out and boarding up burned-down houses. At home, he showed me how to cook and balance my bank statements. All this made me confident I could tackle any type of work thrown my way.

My feelings for my dad were confusing, to put it mildly. I loved him, but was afraid of him. He seemed to know everything and taught me so much, but he also hurt me and messed up my view of a woman's value and role in the world. The wild things we did, like racing cars and riding motorcycles, set me free, but his sexual dominance put me in an internal straitjacket of fear and confusion. He encouraged my sewing and art, but thwarted my inner voice. He taught me to face down fear, yet I feared him. I was scared of him and worshipped him at the same time.

Modeling for photography class in
a dress I made, age fifteen

THE GIRL WHO DRESSES WEIRD

1970s, California

I meet a girl in seventh grade who turns my weird, isolated life inside out. Kelly is my first real friend. She let the kid inside me out of its cage, and that kid is not going back there—ever.

Because friends are not allowed at my house, I go to Kelly's all the time. Her home is completely opposite from mine and filled with peace, love, and laughter. Her parents don't yell, and there's no creepy sex stuff going on. I can't believe it's real. I feel so safe. We talk, listen to albums, mess up the kitchen, and stay up all night laughing. Her parents even say, "Good morning, honey." *Is this for real?*

We run to the cemetery at night and climb the huge oak tree in the middle. Safe, up high in the branches, we smoke a joint and laugh so hard our stomachs hurt. She tells me ghost stories so gruesome we scurry down the tree and run through the creepy granite tombstones (I swear there was fog) all the way to her house. I can't believe my luck—I actually get to do this.

We climb the trees at Golden Park, up high, away from the gang members below, and carve our initials into the branches. We draw cartoon versions of our teachers and go thrift store shopping. Her creativity fuels mine. I go to church with her family, which is totally new for me. My parents hate religion, and my curiosity about God is not tolerated.

Besides my grandmother, Kelly was my first experience with love. She totally changed my life and was the first of so many wonderful friends I have today. I think she saved me. For real.

✦

My parents saved enough money to buy a house in nicer, safer North Downey. It's maybe four miles away, but a totally different world. I have the choice of two high schools because of the move. I go to Warren High, not Downey High like everyone from junior high. I am over the cliques and peer pressure, and think if I go to a new school I can be who I want without other kids talking about it.

With the freedom that comes with anonymity, I bounce into tenth grade as a theme dresser. I am totally unaware of the fact that I am a natural-born fashion designer. I have no idea why I am compelled to design and sew new outfits every day for school.

The hours fly while I sew. I forget to eat and totally lose track of time. Finally, my overactive imagination has a purpose. On Monday I dress as a forties film star, and for the rest of the week it's a fifties housewife, a sailor, a Norwegian dairy farmer, a glam rocker . . . hair and makeup included. For my Bowie glam rock look, I cover my high-heeled platforms in sequins and glitter using toothpicks and glue.

Soon I'm known as "the girl who dresses weird," but I really don't care because I'm having a ball with my creativity. Eventually, the kids get used to it, which is good because I'm not going to stop.

I want to bring Kelly to the Homecoming dance since I'm not ready to date boys. I relish the idea of dressing up like a guy in a tuxedo and top hat. We go to the dance dressed as a couple—me in a suit, bow tie, and top hat, and Kelly in a black dress. The teachers think we're lesbians and forbid us to enter, so we sneak in long enough to have pictures taken. After the photos, three teachers corner us yelling, "You can't come to the dance without a date!" So I say, "She's my date." Our friends gather around, angrily arguing with them. When the teachers threaten to call the police, Kelly and I leave so our friends don't get arrested. Rumors spread that I'm a lesbian, but I really don't give a shit.

The worst part is that after this goes down, my parents forbid me to see my best friend. I'm gutted. I miss her so badly, I cry every night. Once in a while, after my parents are asleep, I sneak out and meet her around the corner to talk, but our relationship is never the same. She can't understand why my parents don't like her and neither can I. Shame colors my emotions. I am powerless to change anything. She is the best, most honest person I had ever known. My longing for her never leaves.

Even with this major loss, I grow in new ways and discover new things. Kissing boys is one, and live rock concerts are another. Because LA is the music capital of the world, every important band comes to town, and I go to as many concerts as possible. Untamed, live rock music sets my soul free, while the outfits worn by David Bowie and Freddie Mercury inspire my imagination and give me permission to be my unique, wildly creative self.

By sixteen, my main goal in life is to move out of the house, so I have two jobs. I teach kids to swim in backyard pools all over Los Angeles County, and I am a salesgirl at a boutique called Nobby's.

◆

At seventeen, I'm about to graduate high school. I want to go to the Fashion Institute of Design and Merchandising (FIDM), but my parents think it is too expensive and that I won't stick with a career in fashion design, so they won't pay for it. Instead, I attend Cerritos community college.

At college, it isn't long before I spot a tall, handsome man in a plaid flannel shirt getting coffee at the campus café. I have a mini heart attack when he asks if he can sit with me. My first serious boyfriend, Jack, is a brilliant machinist, whose lips taste sweet and salty at the same time. He charms the fear of sex right out of me, and I hand him my virginity on a silver platter in the back of his truck at a drive-in movie and naïvely become pregnant right away. I had never gotten a talk about sex or birth control from my mom and was clueless.

I can't tell my parents and have no one to turn to. Jack withdraws. I'm sure he is scared, but I feel totally abandoned. I go to the abortion clinic by USC and lie alone on the cold, stainless steel table, filled with self-hatred and shame. Without painkillers, the doctor pries open my uterus and vacuums it out. I am forever changed. No longer innocent. I'm guilty.

Jack and I continue our relationship using birth control. Yet, he gradually becomes jealous and possessive. He thinks my clothes show too much skin and doesn't want me going to the beach or nightclubs with any of my guy friends. I hate being told what to do, but when I pull away, he holds on tighter—literally. One time he starts jealously yelling at me in his souped-up fast car and begins driving so fast I can't even jump out at a stop sign. When he finally stops the car, he has his muscular hand gripped on my arm so tight I can't move. His controlling behavior pushes me away for a while, but when he comes back crying, I bounce right back into his bed, not really understanding the difference between abuse and love, and furthering my confusion around my own desires and sexuality.

Boating, Marine Stadium, Long Beach, 1978

LA MODEL

1977, Los Angeles Garment District

Nobby's closes, so I waitress at a local deli and work as a box girl at the supermarket. But I yearn for the fashion business. While scanning the want ads in the *Los Angeles Times*, I find one looking for a fit model at a swimwear company. I have no idea what a fit model is, but I go check it out anyway.

High Tide Swimwear is on Broadway in the Los Angeles garment district—a haze of smog, freeway interchanges, and skyscrapers. Homeless people with shopping carts filled with their belongings line the garbage-littered streets. The drab buildings are covered in gang tag graffiti.

Razor wire–topped fencing surrounds my destination and bars cover the windows. I park my red Datsun 240Z sports car on the street in front of the grimy fortress and buzz the intercom at the steel-cage door.

I meet with a red-haired woman named Alleen, who has a thick Texas accent. She's around thirty-five and looks so cool in her tight jeans, high-heeled boots, and long red-fox-fur coat. For some reason, a round faceted crystal from a chandelier is hanging from the buttonhole of her denim shirt. She piques my curiosity.

Her design studio is a bright white room with gray industrial carpet. Rolling racks are jammed with swimsuits, and design sketches are pushpinned to the walls. Colorful marking pens litter her white desk—plus a Styrofoam plate of barbecued ribs, beans, and corn on the cob, and a Coke.

She takes a two-piece off the rack. "Here, darling, try this on, dressing room's in there." She points to a small closet. I put the bikini on and come out. "Oh, you're just a little Lambchop!" (She still calls me this today.) She takes her measuring tape and pulls it up between my legs and over my left shoulder to get a torso measurement. Then she measures the distance between my nipples, plus the more normal bust, waist, and hip numbers.

"You're perfect! I can't believe it! Do you have any idea how many girls I've measured in the past month? This is terrific, I'll call you later today." When she calls later to offer me the job, I negotiate her up from $3.75 to $4.25 per hour.

My job as a fit model is to wear swimsuits while Alleen, or the patternmaker, pins, slices, and writes on them to perfect the design or fit. Alleen works with a lit cigarette hanging on her lip. Her hands tremble as she focuses and talks to the swimsuit. "Come on, you motherfucker," she says, pulling the fabric together, slicing and pinning it.

"Alright, that looks better. Turn around, Lambchop, lemme see the back." Between fittings I wear a hot-pink robe around the office so I'm always ready to change.

When I'm not trying on suits, I cut samples. I hoist massive five-foot-long rolls of fabric on top of my cutting table and arrange pattern pieces efficiently. I use heavy iron weights to keep the pattern pieces from moving. Then I draw around them with a black marker or white tailor's chalk, remove the weights, pin the layers together, and cut them out.

I gather all the trims with the cut pieces and put it all in a plastic Baggie with a Xerox copy of the spec sheet. Now it's time to cut the spaghetti used for neck and back ties. This is a major pain in the ass. The ⅞" by 60" perfectly parallel strips of Lycra are the bane of my existence, because the Lycra runs from my scissors as I cut. My right hand is full of calluses and blisters, but I don't care because I love my job, and I love my mentor, Alleen.

Working at High Tide, I get to see how diverse and inclusive the fashion industry is. Everybody's welcome, whether you're gay, transgender, straight, or from any country on earth. It's just not an issue.

I'm eighteen during my second year at High Tide. We're shooting our ad campaign and my job is to organize and fit suits on twelve models. I'd never been in a real Hollywood photographer's studio, so I'm secretly checking it all out. I'm just a designer's fitting model, not a real photographic model. All of a sudden, I hear rumbling on the set below when Ron Harris, the photographer, fires a model on the spot for being short, then yells up to me in the makeup loft, "Hey, why aren't you in a suit?"

That's how it all started. I shoot the campaign, then ask the president of High Tide to pay me the same amount as the other models and walk away with $800 for a day's work. It's a lot more than $4.25 an hour. If I did this for a living, I think, maybe I can pay for fashion design school at FIDM myself. I have already quit Cerritos College because I am learning so much more working in the garment industry than at school.

I decide to get an agent and meet with four top Hollywood agencies. Three of them want me. I choose the one that I assume does the most photography work. High Tide lets me clock in and out when I have go-sees or bookings, so I still work both jobs and teach swimming on weekends.

My new modeling agency is in Hollywood. Stained dark carpet and fake wood paneling are the design features of the small office. Miriam, the agency head, sits at her desk, her back to the window overlooking the Sunset Strip. Papers and cigarette ash cover her desk. Eight-by-ten, black-and-white model photos are stapled all over the walls. She has dark hair, a strong nose, thick black eyeliner, and a deep, raspy voice.

Apparently, I need all kinds of things done. She sends me to a pediatric cosmetic dentist to have a look at my Tetracycline-stained teeth. The dentist recommends capping them, which means filing my teeth down to a point and putting fake ones on. I can't do it. My teeth have a band of gray, but they are strong and healthy. I feel like I'd be selling out if I had them capped. He bleaches them instead, which in the seventies is terribly painful and doesn't work very well.

Next, a plastic surgeon removes the mole from my chin. He said it could turn cancerous, so I go ahead with it. They want to remove the mole on my cheek too, but I refuse.

Then Miriam sends me to a hairstylist in Beverly Hills named Carlo. I don't know what is in the champagne, but I am so relaxed that night in his salon that I allow him to cut all my hair off into a very short boy cut.

I have no idea that Miriam is the former director of a sexy girls' agency affiliated with a porno magazine. So, naturally, my first interview is with Frederick's of Hollywood. He sells sleazy lingerie. I know this because my parents get the catalog. Miriam comes with me to meet Frederick, who tells me to put on a tiny, see-through, leopard-print thing with black lace trim. I have to change in the closet right next to Frederick's desk, which has shutters for doors that I'm sure he's looking through.

I feel so insanely anxious and uncomfortable with the sleazy outfit and the closet, but I force myself to do it anyway. I come out timidly, basically nude, while Fredrick and Miriam study me up and down and ask me to turn around. I feel like a slut and am panicking internally. Together they agree that though my body is perfect for lingerie, at only eighteen I have too much of a baby face for his product. Thank God.

Miriam books me for cheesy jobs, like car and trucker conventions, where I have to wear a red-white-and-blue, skintight, zip-front polyester jumpsuit. She sends me to hotel and motel rooms all over Hollywood, where clients from out of town hold sketchy interviews.

Sometimes these are not interviews for real jobs. They're just men looking for sex. I go to a house in Bel Air, where a man welcomes me into his lion's den of a home, and, for whatever reason, he has 8×10-inch glossies of girls all over the wall behind his desk, which smells like high-priced hooking to me. My dad has told me of the dozens of times he saved girls like these from overdosing on drugs or on suicide calls—information that stays with me and probably saves me from a bad path in my near future. The man is about forty, with a dark tan, shaggy hair, and chest hair creeping out the top of his shirt. There is no actual product to sell. On second thought, I am the product he wants to sell. He wants to see me in a bikini.

Miriam sends me to a high-rise right on Hollywood and Franklin, where a man, after approving of my body in a bikini, tells me I'll be accompanying him to Las Vegas as his escort. I notice that the man in the photos behind the desk does not match the man in front of me. I try to flee but he has locked me in. I plead desperately for him to unlock the door, he finally relents and I run to the parking garage for my car, telling the security guard about the incident. He couldn't give a shit about my ordeal. I speed out in my car with my heart pounding.

Miriam thinks it would be a good idea for me to go on *The Dating Game*—the seventies game show. Lots of actors use it as a publicity tool. I do it with no intention of looking for a date. My goal is to pick the guy with the least perverted answers. My boyfriend, Jack, who I am trying to break up with at the time, tells me that if I do it our relationship is over—another reason I go on the show.

On an interview for a department store catalog, I meet with a very rare, female photographer. Looking around her studio walls I see fashion shoots, but also sexy shoots. While she looks through my book, she says, "You know, I also shoot for *Oui* [the porno mag-azine] and I'd love to use you." I basically have a silent heart attack and get out of there as fast as I politely can, picturing my dad's gross porno walls at home.

Later, *Oui* magazine calls Miriam offering $25,000 to use a swimsuit shot right out of my portfolio for their cover. I panic. I want the money, but my insides are churning. I don't want the rep-utation of being in pornography magazines! How can I get better jobs for wholesome all-American brands if I let them use my pic-ture? On top of that, the whole thing repulses me because of dealing with my dad's sick porno obsession my whole life. I strongly refuse their offer.

Soon after, I land a national commercial for Sprite and work along a group of other young, fresh-faced athletic actors. I notice that one girl has a look very similar to mine.

When I explain my dilemma with Miriam's sexy go-sees, she suggests I try her agency—Wilhelmina, who recently opened a West Coast branch. Wilhelmina Models in New York is represent-ing some of the biggest names, from Patti Hansen and Gia Carangi to Shaun Casey and Julie Foster.

I want to work in New York someday, and since Wilhelmina has an office there I could easily go. I am dying to shoot with famous New York photographers alongside famous models hot at the time, like Kim Alexis, Carol Alt, Kelly Emberg, Esme Marshall, Beverly Johnson, Janice Dickinson, Iman, Christie Brinkley, Bitten Knud-sen, Tara Shannon, and Brooke Shields.

I go the next day, and they sign me on the spot. The sleazy go-sees disappear, and I model only for legitimate fashion clients: *Cal-ifornia Apparel News*, *Women's Wear Daily*, swimwear companies, department store catalogs, newspaper ads, television commercials, and modeling on talk shows.

I even get invited to glamorous Hollywood parties. My favorite is held at Flipper's, the roller-skating disco in West Hollywood. Patti

Hansen is in our group, along with Robin Williams, who I believe is seeing my agent Molly. *Mork & Mindy* is a hit show at the time, and even Pam Dawber is signed with Wilhelmina. I admit I am startruck.

A few months later, Gerald Marie, the head of Wilhelmina's sister agency, Paris Planning, comes to the US to scout models and he chooses me. My plan is to go to Paris, get editorial tear sheets from *Vogue Paris*, *Elle France*, and every other top magazine, dressed in Paris Couture, of course, then work in New York among my favorite models.

Well, that was the plan.

Wearing Kenzo for the book Fashion
2001 by Lucille Khornak, 1980

STAINED GLASS

March 1980, Paris

It has only been a few weeks since arriving in Paris. Many mornings I head straight to the agency, unless Pepper has already given me my list of go-sees or I am booked for a job. So far, the only jobs I'm getting are the ones I don't want, but I need work and hope that even at a crappy job I can make good connections and move up the slippery steep model ladder.

As I walk into the agency, I feel an instant jolt of tension from the room. Something is seriously wrong. Instead of frenetic buzzing and shouting, it's hushed silence. The mood is dismal. Pepper looks up from her desk, gesturing for me to come over. When I get close she whispers, "Willy has passed away."

"What? How?" I can't believe it. Wilhelmina was only forty and the powerhouse of the agency. How could she be dead?

"Lung cancer. I'll call you later," Pepper says quietly.

I wind down the stairs and go directly to Notre Dame. Magnificent stained glass shines bright in the vast, dim space. Priests' prayers bounce off limestone walls, echoing through the church. I light a candle and kneel.

I think back to my only meeting with Willy and can't get the image of her skeleton fingers and ashy skin out of my head. I didn't know she was sick, but she certainly didn't look well. I wonder how she feels about the fashion business now? Is she glad she spent so much of her life working in fashion? Was it worth the ride? I don't know if God is real, or if he hears me, but I ask him to help me make it in Paris.

I stare at the flickering candles and the beautiful stained glass, thinking, *There's not a single person who really knows me here—not even Scarlett. I'm halfway around the world, so far away from everyone I know. Back home, everybody's got their opinion of who I'm supposed to be, but here, no one has any idea who I am. I have absolutely zero peer pressure. If I change my personality, no one would even notice.* A rush of freedom flows through me. I'm energized. My body feels light. My heart swells. *I can be rude. I can be mean. Maybe I should sleep around or start smoking. I should definitely start cursing. The possibilities are endless.*

I leave the church and on my way back to the hotel, I buy a pack of hand-rolled cigars. As I relax into the sagging hotel mattress, I light one, pondering my options with a wicked smile.

Scarlett and me at Hôtel Andrea, Paris, 1980

HÔTEL ANDREA TO LE BON HÔTEL

Scarlett and I are so excited to pick up our first paychecks at the agency, but when we open the envelopes we're floored. They're much smaller than we had expected. We go directly to the accounting lady downstairs to ask about it. We can barely understand the innocent-looking, petite, Parisian woman saying in broken English something to the effect of "Well, you owe us for the hotel and the plane ticket."

"I thought the agency was paying for that," I say.

"*Non.*"

"But the hotel is so expensive! We never would have chosen to stay there," Scarlett says.

"Sorry . . . *pardon, mais,* I have work to do."

"How much commission do you take out? Because we're only getting maybe thirty percent of our billings," I ask.

"*Zee* agency take twenty percent, *vous payez* fifty percent French tax, and the rest *c'est pour vous.*" She says this like it's no big deal.

We are in shock. Evidently, we had started out in debt to Paris Planning. We thought we had been scouted with a full ride by the agency. And the French taxes! How could they be that much?

I'm lucky to have the $2,400 in traveler's checks to lean on, from selling my car. Scarlett doesn't have a cushion like that. We go straight to the bank to open accounts and deposit our meager checks. I deposit my traveler's checks too so they can't be stolen from our hotel room.

I want to buy clothes that will make me more marketable, but I'm too afraid to spend money. My big splurge is an umbrella and cheap plastic rain boots molded to look like cowboy boots—they're so stupid, but I love them. A badass motorcycle jacket, a plain white T-shirt, cooler jeans, and some real leather boots would have made a huge improvement in my image, but I was far too responsible. Everything is so much more expensive here than at home, and I can't blow my money on clothes when I need food, lodging, photos, and a ticket home. We've got to move to a cheaper hotel.

I find us a tiny room at Hôtel Andrea. It has an armoire for our clothes and a three-foot-square bathroom with a sink and toilet. The shower is down the hall. Our bed, slightly wider than a twin, is opposite the radiator and window that overlooks a courtyard, four stories down. The dark room with the dirty peeling wallpaper, holes in the floor, and rusty sink doesn't bother me. I'm becoming accustomed, even starting to enjoy aging Paris. I unpack my stuff into my half of the armoire and set Scarlett's suitcase on the bed.

We celebrate by going to Les Bains Douche. Being models, the bouncer motions us right into the dark club. When my eyes adjust, I see guys dressed as girls, and girls dressed in vintage, like I do at home. One girl is in a pink, off-the-shoulder, fifties dress with black lace covering her face. She smokes from a long black cigarette holder, with pink Playtex rubber dishwashing gloves. I'm totally jealous of her look.

Scarlett and I jump onto the dance floor, but when we take a break and try to sit down, a woman comes and yells at us. Finally, we figure out that we aren't allowed to sit unless we buy drinks, which we can't afford.

We wander to the other side of the room and see bubbles foaming in a Jacuzzi. A man and woman take off their clothes, climb in, and start having sex. No one seems to think anything of it. We try not to act shocked.

By 3 A.M., we're tiptoeing up our creaky hotel stairs. I turn the skeleton key and open the door to pure warmth. What a relief. Our other hotel never had heat.

Scarlett pulls her suitcase off the bed and climbs under the covers. When I follow her in, the middle of the mattress sinks all the way to the floor. We roll into the middle, laughing and whining at the same time.

"Now I know why this place is so cheap!" she screams.

"I'm sorry, you find the next one. I'm obviously bad at this!"

I throw my leg over the edge, clinging to the side of the bed, while Scarlett sleeps in the middle. But we always wake up tangled in the ditch.

With all the deductions the agency takes out of my paychecks, I have to make three times the money I made in Los Angeles just to survive. Catalog jobs are easy and pay better than magazine work, which I am not getting much of anyway. On catalog jobs I make around a thousand dollars a day—even though I only receive a small percentage of that. Magazines only pay around twenty-five dollars a day, even *Vogue*. I don't care if I get paid a big fat zero if it's shooting for *Vogue*! But I'm not.

The biggest mail-order company in Europe, 3 Suisses, sends me by train to work in towns all over France and Belgium. I rise before dawn, with Scarlett still asleep. She stays up late reading romance novels in the tiny bathroom, so as not to disturb my sleep. It isn't easy living in such close quarters, especially when we're sleeping on top of each other. I try not to wake her as I leave.

Freezing winter air hits my face. The only people crazy enough to be out this early are the café waiters who are busy hosing off the sidewalk and the prostitutes who hang around the train station. Other than them, it's silent.

I stare up at the massive Gare du Nord structure, trying to imagine what it would look like if someone cleaned the grime off. I can picture a beautiful cathedral of sculpted metal and glass.

A first-class ticket to Brussels costs slightly more than the regular fare but is totally worth it. It includes a seat in the dining car at a table with white linen tablecloths. After the train departs, a waiter serves me a café crème and a warm, flaky, buttery croissant. I write postcards and absorb the beauty outside my window. Fields of bright green, tall, wet grass and charming farmhouses seem right out of a fairy tale.

The one and only challenge of catalog work is the sheer volume of clothing that needs to be shot. Two women work all day long, steaming and ironing garments within an inch of their lives, while I am pinned and duct-taped to hide the wrinkles. Then I pose, stomach in, shoulders back, and wait for the shutter to click and the lights to pop.

Look left; look right; look straight at the camera like I'm enjoying the hell out of these ugly clothes. These pictures will not go in my book, but I love the clients. They pay me well, feed me, and even put me up in an adorable hotel that I could never afford to stay in on my own.

After five days of work, I take the train home from Brussels and arrive at Paris's Gare du Nord around midnight and board the bus along with all the other immigrants, back to my neighborhood. I'm exhausted and my whole body hurts from holding those stupidly unnatural catalog poses, but I feel productive after doing a big job instead of going on endless go-sees. I feel a sense of accomplishment, and the money makes me feel safe. As I finally sink into the ditch of our bed and wrap up in the thin red blanket, I realize that I'm actually happy. I'm creating my own life in Paris and, even though it's not perfect, I'm doing it my way and I love it.

Scarlett focuses on finding us a better hotel, even splurging on real bath towels for both of us. Our new place, Le Bon Hôtel, is near the Seine, with a view of Notre Dame if you lean out the window. The room is bright and sunny, but the best feature is two separate beds. No toilet though, so we're back to peeing in the bidet.

It's been over two months of Pepper's second-tier castings and catalog work. I thought I'd be gone by now. And since I won't go to their parties, Gerald refuses to help me get magazine editorial. I decide to have a serious talk with him. He holds the power, not Pepper. I fret about what to say as I go about my morning routine.

A huge Saint Bernard naps in the doorway of my favorite café. I pet him, speaking to him in French, but he just ignores me. I step over him to get inside. The waiters, who a couple months earlier were pissed off at me for not speaking French, now teach me new words every day. They generously write them on my paper placemat, sounding them out over and over for me. I tear them out and keep the word scraps in my purse until I've got them memorized. My grammar isn't as good as my vocabulary, but I'm getting around much better.

I sit with my café au lait and hard-boiled egg, as I practice what to say to Gerald—a million versions of "you're not taking me seriously."

I rehearse my speech all the way to the agency, march in the door, and wait in front of his station. Finally, he gets off the phone.

"*Pardon*, Gerald? *Puis, je—vous parler?*" I ask if I can talk with him.

"*Oui, qu'est-ce que vous voulez chérie?*" He asks me what I want in a sweet tone that takes me totally by surprise.

"Gerald, nothing against Pepper, but I haven't been on magazine go-sees in weeks. Can't Jacqueline and Evelyn and *you* book me again?"

"*Oui, chérie*, why not? I will send you to the big magazines again. There is absolutely no reason why you shouldn't make it in Paris, Gilles. I will work you very hard until the end of April. If by then you still don't have the right amount of work, I will send you to

Milan. I am behind you, *chérie.*" He smiles that wide smile, where even the smile lines at the sides of his blue eyes smile too.

He's done punishing me for complaining about the parties. Or maybe it's just because my hair has grown out from its hideous phase. I immediately land a shoot for *Jardin des Modes,* one of France's best fashion magazines.

Risking our lives for the perfect editorial shot!
That's me on the top left. Jardin des Modes

JARDIN DES MODES

Eighteen models, including me, meet at *Jardin des Modes*'s office at 10 rue Thenard at 5 A.M. The room is packed with models, stylists, makeup artists, and hairstylists. I love everything about this whole scene. I check out the rolling racks crammed with colorful dresses and feel totally honored to be looking at each one. No one else seems to be as obsessed with the clothes as I am. I read every tag on the rack—Yves Saint Laurent, Jean-Paul Gaultier, Claude Montana, Thierry Mugler, Issey Miyake, Sonia Rykiel . . . I can't believe it— finally. Paris Couture!

The next two hours are a flurry of activity. The fashion editor chooses which designer dress each of us will wear, while at least a dozen hair and makeup artists attack us with foundation, colored shadows, eyeliner, lipstick, curling irons, hairpins, gel, and hairspray.

I love the dress the editor picks for me—a Jean Claude de Luca Couture lace corset tutu with yellow embroidery. When the final touches of accessories are complete, we all cram into white vans and race through the still quiet, dark, foggy streets. We are let out at the Place du Trocadéro apex between the two wings of the Palais de Chaillot, which creates the perfect frame for the Eiffel Tower just beyond.

There's obviously a construction project going on because there is a tall scaffolding structure. The photographer, Michel Momy, takes out a megaphone and directs all of us to climb the scaffolding. This command was met with a lot of "Hell no!" "I'm not climbing that!" "Is he crazy?" But I can't wait to climb it.

Realizing this is the shot he wants and there is no way out, the girls finally relent and we all climb the metal structure in heels and gowns, while Michel sets up his camera equipment. The foggy air is drizzling and freezing cold. Everyone is screaming and slipping on the poles, hanging on tight to not fall off. We are up at least fifty feet in the air. One of the girls, from Louisiana, cries in her southern accent, "I'm freezin' and I'm bleedin'! This metal dress is cuttin' me all over!" *Drama queen*, I think.

With Michel directing us into position, yelling at us through his megaphone, we climb and shinny into place. Finally, he starts shooting. Just as we get going though, a crew of angry, macho construction men arrives. They wave their arms in Michel's face, trying to block his camera! They're obviously pissed off. He ducks and dodges trying to shoot around them. Eventually, he picks up his megaphone and orders us to come down. We descend the wet slippery poles, and when we reach solid ground we break out in nervous, relieved laughter.

We pile back in the van, huddling together, shivering. The poor girl from Louisiana is dripping with blood from that gold lamé dress.

Wearing Jean Claude de Luca on the Seine for
Fashion 2001 by Lucille Khornak, 1980

LE PALACE

At the time, I was totally unaware of Gerald's reputation.

What I know now is a different story. There are a pile of articles, books, and stories you can easily find about his deplorable behavior, including accusations of rape. But I didn't know any of that then.

So I am thrilled when he invites Scarlett and me out dancing at Le Palace, the popular nightclub. The massive dance floor is packed when we arrive. A glowing thirty-foot mermaid is rolled onto the stage as bubbles fall from the ceiling. I am trying to learn the new eighties dance moves, but Gerald has them totally mastered, and looks so damn sexy in his black leather motorcycle jacket.

The three of us return to Gerald's apartment around 4 A.M., where he indulges us with soft music and drinks. *Where is my moody boss?* I relish the pampering and attention.

Suddenly, Scarlett stands up and says she's leaving. "Are you coming, *Jill?*" with emphasis on the *Jill.*

"No, you go ahead. I'll see you at home." I kiss her cheeks and she whispers, "Come with me. Seriously. Now." I had no appreciation for her wisdom and foresight then, only thinking to myself: *How dare she tell me what to do.*

I whisper back, "I'm gonna stay awhile. I'll be home soon." Gerald didn't stand up to say good-bye to Scarlett or even offer a taxi.

I tell myself she'll be fine. After all, we walk around alone at night all the time.

Gerald and I are sitting talking on the steps between his living room and hall when he leans in to kiss me with his warm, soft lips. I haven't been kissed in months—certainly not like that. His kisses make me feel drunk, even though I haven't had a drop of alcohol. After a while, he stands up. "Can I make you a bath, *chérie?*" he offers, opening a door to reveal a beautiful marble bathtub.

"Oh, god yes!" I say. I'm sleepy, not to mention naïve. And I really want a hot bath. As he turns on the water, I recline on a velvet couch, thinking, *So this is how a French person with money lives—nice apartment, velvet furniture, fireplace, stereo system, even a refrigerator.* I am seduced by the luxury of it all.

"Gilles, your bath is ready, come." The room smells like lavender and honey. Bubbles spill over the side and sparkle in the candlelight. I can't believe it. He goes to his bedroom next to the bathroom. "I'll be watching television. I left you a robe. Why are you standing there, you don't like it?"

"No, I love it. I just can't believe it. It's beautiful, I'm getting in."

He watches me take my clothes off. I try to pretend I'm at a photo shoot, where I'm comfortable being naked. I step in, sink down, and feel every inch of my body relax. I lie submerged up to my chin until I almost fall asleep.

I get up slowly as the blood rushes to my head. I dry off and wrap myself in the white terry cloth robe.

"Come watch American television with me. It's a Western, you know John Wayne?"

"What? You're kidding!"

"No, look!"

I edge into his bedroom, hair dripping, my body warm and rosy. His bed is on the floor with white sheets and a fluffy white down comforter. Piles of pillows line the wall where he rests his head. He opens the blankets for me and I climb in nervously, trying to focus on the French John Wayne movie. It's in black and white, and the high-pitched French voice they use to dub John Wayne is ridiculous. I can't stop giggling.

After a few minutes, Gerald turns and kisses me and I melt again, relishing his tenderness. I'm lost in my fantasy of a romantic haze, when all of a sudden he grabs my hips and flips me onto my stomach. He quickly gets behind me and pulls me up from behind, so I'm on my elbows and knees. It happened so fast, and before I can catch my breath or say a word he shoves himself inside me, thrusting crazily, digging his fingernails into my flesh, thrashing me around hard, and hurting me. His hands grip my hipbones so tight I can't move or get him to stop.

"Oww! Stop!" I scream, but he won't stop until he comes inside me. Then he flips over and lays there, satisfied. I'm paralyzed. My body is buzzing all over, even my ears buzz. My first thought is *Oh god, I'm pregnant.*

Gerald passes out while I lie numb and confused, my eyes wide open in the dark, tears trailing down into my ears. Hours pass, and the pillow soaks. Finally, a little light starts beaming through the window over our heads.

I roll out of the bed and creep into the bathroom to find my clothes. I have to pee so badly, but I can't relax my bladder enough to go. Gerald lays there, sleeping soundly, as I tiptoe out his door.

I walk home in pain, and can't tell what hurts worse: my bladder, vagina, or mind. The sun isn't up all the way and everything is gray. The air is gray, the buildings are gray, the streets are gray, even the trees are gray. I am gray. I can't hear a sound. I can't feel the cold. I can barely focus my eyes. I put one foot ahead of the other. I try to separate from my body. Don't panic, keep quiet, stay still inside, and keep walking.

The next three days are a blur as I peel back each layer of shock. I can't accept the truth of what happened, so I twist the story line around in my head. I'm a pro at this due to my childhood. I tell myself that he acted that way because he was nervous or maybe got too excited. It could mean that Frenchmen are just lousy lovers. He was a good kisser. . . . Maybe he really likes me.

At the agency, Pepper gives me the great news that I got the Vittel water commercial and I'm going to Saint-Tropez to film. As I turn around, Gerald is coming straight toward me with his big smile, blue eyes, and gorgeous tanned smile lines, and he's looking me right in the eyes. He kisses my cheeks slowly and passionately, hugs me tight, and takes my shoulders in his hands, pulling me close, saying, "You know, Gilles, I have been thinking to have a girl-friend, yes? What do you think? I am ready for a girlfriend, no?" The agency is deserted. It is just him and me, and Pepper behind me.

"Really? You want a girlfriend?" I laugh, but my face is flushed with flattery. What if he were my boyfriend? I'd have a lover, a friend, and a charming man to go on dates with. Then a selfish, calculating thought pops into my head. Gerald Marie is the most powerful modeling agent in France.

"Let's go for a walk, *chérie*, and have some tea." He places his hand on the small of my back, leading me outside. My heart races as we stroll down rue Tronchet toward the Champs-Élysées. I'm so happy and feel so special! I imagine how different my life could be with Gerald in it. First of all, I wouldn't be alone. And the whole work situation would be solved instantly. He'd book me for the best jobs in Paris—covers of *Vogue, Elle*. . . . I'm jittery and nervous. He is so damn handsome too! The violence of the other night has faded, put away in the face of sudden belonging and the comfort of being *wanted*.

It's spring, the air is crisp, but the sun feels warm. We sit at an outdoor café on the Champs-Élysées, sharing a pot of tea and watching the parade of people pass by.

"People are really ugly, aren't they?" he says, crinkling his face.

"What do you mean?"

"Just look at them!" he says.

"They're just people."

"I spend so much time in the agency, I guess I never see regular people . . . they're horrible-looking."

"I think you need to get out more," I say laughing.

"Maybe." He shrugs, moving on. "Anyway. You know, maybe I should have a girlfriend. You could be my girlfriend, Gilles. I am ready to be monogamous. One woman. What do you think?"

"Sure, I guess we could try it."

"*Oui*, okay then, *garçon*—" He pays the bill, and we stand up. He hugs me tight and holds me close all the way back to the agency.

While I gather my mail, I whisper to Pepper, asking for the phone number of a doctor who could give me birth control. On my way out, Gerald hands me a note that reads,

> *Be good while you're gone!*
> *Love,*
> *Gerald*

I go to Pepper's doctor, who gives me a prescription for a diaphragm. I haven't had a period since arriving in Paris, so he also gives me a pill that is supposed to give me my period. At the time, I think the lack of a period is due to the change in drinking water, but in reality, I'm not eating enough.

✦

I do some of my best thinking on airplanes, and on the flight to Saint-Tropez I think about Gerald. One minute I'm excited, the next I'm wondering if he is actually serious about a relationship. I flash back to the night in his bed, hoping that over time he could become a better lover.

A crew member drives me from the airport to the hotel in warm, sunny Saint-Tropez. I push open the wood shutters in my room to take in the view of the harbor filled with boats and the hillsides covered in orange and purple wildflowers. Even the floral bedding is sunny and bright.

I plop on the bed to enjoy my gorgeous surroundings when the unrelenting questions invade my peace: *Am I pregnant? What was that pill the doctor gave me? If I'm pregnant, my career is over. How will I survive? Who can I lean on? I can't run home to my parents. Would Gerald be there for me?*

That evening, I meet the film crew and other actors in the hotel restaurant downstairs. While I sit among them, I feel like my world is slowly caving in. Tunnel vision takes over and I start to obsess over the conversations that I cannot fully understand.

I become paranoid, thinking they are saying bad things about me. Insecurity takes over, and when they laugh I think they are laughing at me. I feel like a total outsider and can't shake this awful state of mind. To top it all off, the other actress there has every physical trait that I not only want but need, from her narrow hips and long hair to her perfect white teeth. It drives me crazy. As filming begins, I suck it up and work as a professional, singing and dancing my heart out in that stupid black-and-white waitress costume. But inside I'm a mess.

After a week of shooting, I am relieved to return to gray, rainy Paris. When I walk into our hotel room, Scarlett is standing in front of the open windows, smoking. She only smokes when she's stressed. She turns around and says, "Look, I don't have to tell you this, but while you were gone Gerald tried to sleep with me. I didn't do it, but next time I might. Just giving you a heads-up." She turns back around to face the city.

Scarlett's honesty made Gerald's character immediately obvious, and in a split second my heart ricochets from excited to see him, to I never want to see his fucking face again.

"You know what, Scarlett?" I spit. "If that's how he is, I don't want him. Help yourself."

How could she put a man before our friendship? Does she want sex or help with modeling? And was Gerald trying to play us both at the same time? Maybe he thinks it's fun trying to pit us against each other? It doesn't matter either way. I'm not here for love. I'm here for tear sheets from *Vogue Paris*.

Next time I'm in the agency, I make it clear that I'm not going to play Gerald's games. After thinking through my various options, I decide to totally ignore him because I don't have the guts or self-confidence to tell him how I really feel. My inner rage must have filled the entire room.

The next day, Pepper motions me to her desk and says, "I'll be handling you. Empty your book."

"What? Why?"

"Take your pictures out. You're getting a 'Talents' book." Talents is the name of their amateur agency. I go from a bright white Paris Planning portfolio to a cheap brown Talents one.

I'm humiliated and feel like I've been stabbed in the chest. Gerald obviously doesn't like being ignored. Now my own agency is working against me. I feel powerless.

Paris courtyard, 1980

BROKEN BOUNDARIES

I was a wide-eyed girl, excited to grow up and be independent. I didn't have a clue that my natural instincts and protective inner voice had been destroyed. I didn't know how to stand up for myself or say no—especially to someone in authority. I didn't even realize I had been traumatized and needed to heal. My traumas sat brewing and stewing inside me for years, coloring and influencing my decisions as I unknowingly brought myself into duplicate scenarios. My friendly, trusting, and naïve nature was instantly apparent to the wrong kind of men, the ones who would use love to take advantage of me.

I justified Gerald's horrible behavior. I didn't know what else to do. Today, I understand. Living day after day and year after year in an environment where rules change by the hour and personal boundaries are never respected has a profound result. Children growing up in oversexualized homes or who are physically or emotionally abused (many much worse than me) are damaged and, many times, forever affected.

While researching for this book, I read laws from child welfare government websites, such as the Child Welfare Information Gateway and the National Child Traumatic Stress Network. I learned that sexual abuse includes both touching and non-touching behaviors. When I read about the effect this has on children, everything finally made sense. It has helped me to stop beating myself up over my bad decisions, lack of healthy boundaries, character misjudgments, and re-victimizations. With shame clouding my view I was two separate people—a bold, free-spirited girl on the outside and an easily manipulated girl on the inside.

Pretending I smoke in Paris, 1980

THE ROAD TO PUERTO BANÚS

On Friday night Pepper calls my hotel, something she never does. "Jill, it's Pepper. You're going to London right now!" she screams.

I switch into work mode. "I don't have much cash and the banks are closed until Monday!"

"You'll be fine. Swing by the agency. I've got your ticket. See you soon."

I race over in a taxi, and Pepper hands me a plane ticket through the car window, mentioning the job is for an English trench coat company. The taxi speeds toward the airport, but we hit a huge traffic jam on the freeway from a Bob Marley concert. I sit stressed out in the backseat for two hours and miss my flight. I don't have money for another taxi home and back, so I wait in the airport overnight for the first flight to London in the morning.

Airport terminals have become kind of a second home to me. I know that's weird, but I've got my rituals. I buy a magazine and a decaf café au lait for dinner. I know where the comfortable chairs are. I sit and write in my journal and study French.

I decipher the magazine, while trying to ignore the staring perverts. I'm getting good at tuning them out. I'm always ready now to get up in their face and challenge them: "Do you have a problem?" or "Why are you staring at me? Please stop." In French, in a super-serious tone. I even tell them off in crowded restaurants, which they seem to find embarrassing. The other men in the restaurant usually giggle. Serves them right, I say.

When I first arrived in Paris, there was a wall isolating me from the people I lived among. It took so much energy just to get food or water or find a bathroom. I wasn't working in an office with a coffee machine, a sink that provides water, or a bathroom for employees. I basically worked outside, walking the streets all day to go-sees and interviews, among unfamiliar surroundings and a total language barrier.

The French in 1980 didn't have the patience to deal with me and my lack of fluency. Learning to properly say "water" or "egg" was such a challenge. Those two simple words that could sustain me were so hard to pronounce. Even if the café employees knew that I wanted an egg, if I mispronounced it, they would shake their heads and ignore me.

But now, after breaking the French code, I find pleasure translating and learning my new language. I carry a tiny French-to-English dictionary, smaller than a pack of cigarettes. I write words I don't know in the margins of magazines and look them up later. If it's an article I want to understand right away, I translate as I go. I write down the word and definition, tear the pages out, and carry them with me until the words are memorized. It's no longer a burden. I actually enjoy it. Becoming more comfortable and fluent gave me a stronger sense of confidence and freedom to live my new life in Paris—and what I didn't fully realize then was how huge that was toward my independence and self-worth.

◆

Finally, I curl up on the floor, under a row of chairs in the waiting area, and sleep with my bag as a pillow like the homeless do.

London is covered in fog, exactly how I expect it to be. I pay the cabdriver and rush to the address Pepper has given me, where the office door opens to two men. "You the girl from Paris?" the man behind the desk asks.

"Yes." I'm tired.

"We're flying to Spain," he says.

"Are you the photographer, Brian Westley?" I ask.

"Who else would I be?" he says in a thick British accent. *Smart-ass. I'm not ready to deal with his attitude. I just want to do my job and go home.*

"My agent said the job was here in London. I missed my flight last night and had to sleep in the airport." It felt odd to speak English with a client.

"Well, I've changed my mind—working on my pilot's license. We're shooting in Marbella, Spain. You'll fly with me," he says.

An alarm goes off in my head. "No, thanks. I don't fly in small private planes. I'll catch a flight and meet you there." *Oh shit. Here we go again.*

He looks pissed. "You're not getting it, sweetie. Part of the job is to fly with me."

I'm ready to walk out on this whole thing, but give him one last chance. "Just give me the name of the hotel and I'll meet you there. Oh, and I'm out of money, so can I have cab fare to the airport, please?"

For some reason, he backs down and hands me the hotel address in Spain, picks up the phone, and books me a flight. He even gives me cab money, and I return to the airport, where I sit for hours practicing my French, waiting for the night flight to the Málaga airport.

I arrive in Spain around 2 A.M. Riding in a taxi along the coast, I see an enormous silhouette of a black bull on top of a hill. I wonder why this ominous beast is up there. Maybe it is my mood, or the lack of food, or sleep, but it feels like a bad omen. (Now, I know it is a forty-six-foot-high billboard for Osborne Spanish brandy, and these advertising bulls are all over Spain.) The cab radio keeps repeating *"Puerto Banús . . ."* over and over, but I can't understand the rest of what is said. I pay the driver with my remaining change, surely shortchanging him.

I ask for a room key at the front desk.

"I am sorry, *señorita*, we have no reservation for you. A different name perhaps?"

"Brian Westley? But I have my own room," I say, exasperated.

"The reservation says two people in one room. Will you like me to show you your room?" he says.

Should have seen that coming. "No, *gracias*. Can I have another room under his reservation? I've been traveling for two days and really need to sleep." I am at the end of my rope.

"I am sorry, we are fully booked. When he arrives, you speak with him." I give up.

I just curl up in a chair in the lobby when I overhear a group of people speaking English—American English. They're in the bar, so I decide to go over, hoping for food. "Hi, I'm so happy to hear someone speak English."

"Oh, are you American too?" the only girl asks.

"Yeah, I'm from California."

"Do you wanna sit?" one of the men asks.

I'm trying not to stare at the sandwiches. "Yes, thank you. What are you all doing in Spain?"

"We work on a boat, but the port's been evacuated. Bomb threat," one of them says.

"What?" What could possibly happen next?

The man who seems in charge says, "The prince of Belgium is supposed to arrive, and a terrorist group wants to bomb his boat. I'm Captain Terry, by the way. Help yourself to the sandwiches." The captain looks to be in his mid-forties, tanned, weathered from the sea.

Food, thank goodness. "I'm Jill. That's terrible!" I carefully take a sandwich and bite into it. "So, do all of you work on the boat?" There are around a dozen in the crew, and the handsome one with dark hair and blue eyes says, "Yeah, we work for the prince, driving the boat port to port, wherever he wants it. And what are you doing here? Oh, and I'm Mark." He looks preppy in his navy polo and khaki shorts. I feel comfortable and safe with them, having grown up around waterskiing boats. It feels like a common thread.

The man from the front desk runs over to the captain. "The hotel has just received a bomb threat. They know the prince's crew is here." He starts panicking, waving his arms. "You all must leave immediately!" I tell Mark I'm waiting for a photographer but don't want to stick around for a bomb.

"Mark, could I come with you guys, please?" I beg.

"Gotta ask the captain."

The captain has overheard. "Okay. Act like you're part of the crew."

Machine gun–toting soldiers lead us in the dark through mud and bushes to a different hotel. We crouch down and walk low to the ground to avoid being seen, all while tripping on branches and rocks and getting stuck in mudholes. The only lights are a few flashlights that the soldiers carry. It is totally surreal. We go directly to the bar, down shots of tequila, and dance like this is our last night alive.

At about 4 A.M., Mark says, "You can sleep in my room. . . ."

The captain must have seen the panic flash over my face, and he jumps in, "There's a spare bed in my room, Jill. That might make you comfortable."

"That sounds good, thank you," I say.

When I awake in the morning, the captain is dressed and heading out the door. I call Brian, the photographer, to see if he's arrived at the other hotel.

He is irate. "Where are you? Why weren't you in my room last night?"

"There was a bomb threat. I had to leave the hotel," I explain.

"I want you here now. I'll be at the pool." He hangs up.

Oh boy, here we go. . . .

The sun is scorching already, so I throw on my shorts and walk back to the first hotel, on the road this time, not through the bushes. Every single car honked at me the entire way, probably thinking I was a prostitute, which is a nice way to start the day. Brian is at the pool, sunbathing with his flight instructor, Todd, and Todd's girlfriend.

"When are we shooting?" I'm all sweaty.

"Errr, I don't feel like shooting today. Get changed and come lie by the pool." He's sprawled out in a stupid red Speedo and mirrored sunglasses. His bald head and big, hard belly are slathered and shiny with tanning oil. His teeth are jagged and tobacco-stained. A wide scar stretches under his chin along his neck and up to his ear—like a knife wound.

"Why don't you go to the hotel shop and buy yourself something? Charge it to my room." He guzzles a beer.

"No, thanks, I'm good," I say.

"Go ahead. Buy yourself a swimsuit or a dress. Bill it to the room, lovey," he pushes.

He is gross and disgusting, and I say, "Nothing's free," and walk back to the lobby.

Later in the day, he promises to get me my own room after we eat dinner. I dress for dinner, leaving my bag in his room for the time being. "You know I won't be sleeping here, right?" I repeat.

It is so hard to understand their thick British accents over dinner. Brian keeps ordering drinks for me, and by the end of dinner I am thoroughly trashed. My lack of sleep isn't helping either.

Back at the hotel, I follow him to his room to grab my stuff, saying, "Don't forget, I still need you to get me my own room."

"Yeah, I will. . . ."

Once we're in, he closes the door and says, "You're being ridiculous, Jill. It's late. Just sleep here. I won't touch you. Look, we have two beds." I'm drunk, tired, and tired of fighting, so I slip into one of the beds.

Just as I'm nodding off, he startles me awake by sitting on top of my ass with his hairy, disgusting ball sac dangling between my thighs. He digs his hands into my shoulders in a pseudomassage. I freak out. Some crazy, superhuman strength comes over me, and I thrust him off.

"Give me my fucking ticket!" I yell with a force I didn't know I possessed. My words feel like lightning bolts jolting out at him. He looks as though something has shoved him against the wall.

"Look, let's start over and forget any of this ever happened," he begs. "Please, let's pretend you just got here. Please calm down."

I could see him eyeing his briefcase, so I dart over and grab my ticket from the outside pocket and run out the door. He's naked, so I've got a head start. I push the elevator button, but he's running, so I bolt down the stairs. I must have run down six stories without looking back.

I beg for my passport at the front desk, and I turn around and see him emerging from the elevator. As I run for the valet, I turn to catch a glimpse of him running at me in his Speedo with his robe flapping, yelling, "Come back, let's start over!"

I jump in the taxi yelling, "*Puerto Banús! Puerto Banús, por favor!*" The only thing I know to say, from the radio.

He takes off, but begins arguing with me in Spanish about something, saying, "*No no! Puerto Banús—la bomba!*"

I keep looking back behind us on the road, sure that Brian is chasing us. The driver keeps warning me in Spanish, and I wish to God that I'd taken it in high school so I could understand him. Thankfully, he keeps driving. He eventually and reluctantly drops me between three massive army tanks that are blocking the entrance to Puerto Banús. I have no money, so I bolt from the car, crying out, "*Gracias, señor!* I'm so sorry!"

I run through the twisting streets toward the water. I'm still worried Brian is following me, so I zigzag all the way to the sand. Finally, I reach the beach and plop on a lounge chair. I lie back, look up at the stars, and try to calm the fuck down. I tell myself, *I'm okay, I wasn't raped. I'm gonna be alright.* I think about the fact that if something really terrible had happened and I disappeared, no one would notice for a long time and wouldn't know where to start looking. The agency doesn't even know I'm in Spain.

Soldiers patrol the beach, machine guns swinging from their hips. *Great, a bunch of guys in the dark with guns. I'm going to be attacked by the Spanish army.* As I try to get that thought out of my head and focus on the stars, a big German shepherd, like a police dog, comes over by me. I hope he's not vicious. He's not. He curls up next to my lounge on the sand and protects me all night long, barking at the men patrolling the beach and laying back down next to me.

While I stare up at the sky full of stars, I'm sure that something is watching over me. How else could I have escaped? What was that bolt of energy that threw the photographer across the room? That definitely wasn't me. If we live among angels, I think one just shoved that dude against the wall. I start to grasp the strange reality that some powerful force has the whole situation under control. I've never felt this way in my life. I'm in awe and, by some strange miracle, I feel totally at peace. I stare at the stars, feeling more alive than ever.

In the morning, I decide that I'm not running back to Paris screaming "victim." Instead, I will take care of myself by staying in Spain for a much-needed vacation. I have my Visa card with me for emergencies only, and my need for a break is an emergency right now. I book a room at the hotel I stayed in with Captain Terry and the crew the night of the bomb threat. Since I don't have any cash, I charge everything I eat or need to the hotel because they keep my credit card. For the next eight days I relax, pondering the feeling that I am being looked over.

I swim, lie in the sun, and even have dinner with Mark, the cute guy from the crew of the prince's yacht. One morning, wandering through the village, the aroma of freshly baked bread wafts through the air. When the baker notices me, he comes out of his stall to offer me a loaf. I say, "No money," showing him my empty palms;

he smiles, looks into my eyes, and puts the small, warm loaf in my hands. Nothing ever tasted so good.

Back in Paris, at the agency, Pepper isn't surprised when I tell her what happened. She calls London, demanding payment for the job. Of course, I never get paid. I bet Brian wasn't even a real photographer. I never saw those trench coats I was supposed to model either.

✦

The inner peace that hit me on that beach in Spain had my attention, and when I got back to Paris it didn't stop. I had a new perspective on life. Nothing was more important than retaining the peace in my soul. A near-rape experience was a weird way to get peace, but whatever. I was sure of one thing: It didn't come from me. It came from something more powerful than me. I began going to the gorgeous cathedrals more often, lighting candles and praying. I didn't have a clue how to pray, and was positive that I was doing it wrong. I just didn't want the peace inside to fade away.

The experience in Spain has changed me. Not the gross guy in the Speedo, but the bolt of energy that came from inside me and the dog that watched over me all night. If some good, protective power knows where I am, then maybe I should relax and stop worrying.

I decide to immediately stop obsessing over modeling, and instead focus on making a peaceful, happy life for myself. Being protected and cared for in Spain gives me the confidence to loosen up my budget, so I begin my new worry-free life by purchasing a Walkman, even though it's five hundred dollars. It is a huge splurge. I use some of the money I had brought with me to Paris from selling my car in California. I need to have music back in my life. I buy cassette tapes and blast Queen, Bowie, and Roxy Music into my ears while I walk all over Paris and everywhere else I go.

Then, I make another huge shift. Instead of using the dirty, dark Metro, I figure out how to ride the bus, which gives me a front-row seat to the beauty of Paris. I am literally out of the dark, and into the light.

I stop checking in with Paris Planning for constant updates. Instead of thinking about Gerald and Pepper, I do what I want.

I waste hours on purpose, reading novels at the English bookstore WH Smith on rue Rivoli in its cozy upstairs tearoom, dipping biscuits in hot tea, knowing this is what I choose to do instead of worrying about work. I wander through all the different flea markets, searching for treasures. I buy flea market clothes that suit my personality instead of guessing what the agency wants me to wear.

I even change my eating habits. I seek out and discover new, delicious food. I start eating things I refused to eat before, so worried about gaining a pound. I enjoy apricot crepes overflowing with whipped cream instead of starving myself; *salade vert* with mustard dressing; shredded celery root with mayonnaise; pizza topped with a fried egg; and Kir, wine with crème de cassis. I discover a vegetarian restaurant, where I can get baked vegetables topped with golden-brown, melted cheese. I even eat chocolate bars with hazelnuts. I treat myself and buy flowers at the big flower stand by the Madeleine Church.

Scarlett and I hang out at the park on weekends with bread, wine, cheese, and a blanket. We go to the Louvre and the Pompidou. My life is not on hold. I'm here now, living in the present.

The noise of the city is the background music for my peace of mind while I sit in cafés or walk for miles. I listen to my thoughts. They're simple, profound, and peaceful.

Sometimes it's a conversation, and sometimes I hear a voice. I'm a world away from everything I've ever known before and am falling more in love with Paris every day.

I stop to watch the old ladies feed pigeons in the park. I get to know café owners and study the beauty of the foam on my café au lait. Have you ever really looked at the simple beauty of a pure white sugar cube? How, when the sun reflects on it, it sparkles like a cluster of diamonds? I slow myself down to enjoy each moment, knowing I may never have another quite like it.

Red wine baby bottles, Montmartre, Paris, 1980

DREAMING IN FRENCH

Pepper seems to get more pleasure from hanging out with me than she does from promoting me. It is hard to keep friendships with my model friends because all of us are always in and out of town, yet Pepper is always here working. We go to lunch together often at Le Roi du Pot au Feu, across from the agency, where I have a front-row seat to her cabaret of sexually charged flirting and exaggerated French. I hate to admit it, but I actually love the sound of her voice. It's entertaining, to say the least.

As we walk in, the men behind the bar shout, "*Bonjour, petite Poivre et grande Gilles!*" (Hello, little Pepper and tall Jill!) It is a typical French bistro, with wallpaper on the top half of the wall and wood paneling on the lower. It has black leather booths and small black and white hexagon tiles on the floor. Wineglasses hang from brass tubing over the zinc bar. The vibe is always friendly and happy here. The waiter brings us red wine and water and already knows we're having the stew.

"Oh, Jill, if you'd be willing to cut your hair super short, I've got a great editorial job for you," Pepper says.

"Seriously? I can't. It's finally getting longer!" I say.

"Yeah, I get it. Okay."

"Why does every good shoot have something difficult about it?"

"I don't know. . . . This business is crazy."

"So, what brought you to Paris originally, *petite* Poivre?" I ask in my half-English, half-French way.

"To teach English at the Sorbonne," she says.

This sounds like a bullshit answer. She's damaged. I think she uses her overly perfect French to mask a dark secret, and I want to know what it is. "Wow. The Sorbonne? How long were you planning to stay?"

She looks at the men at the bar. "I don't know." She drinks her wine, lights a cigarette.

I keep going. I've got nothing to lose. Neither she nor Gerald care about me. I'm just commissions to them. "Did you speak French when you got here?"

"No." She holds up the empty wine carafe, jiggling it, signaling for more. "I learned it over time."

"How about your family in the US?" I lean in and pick at the bread.

She looks right at me. "What family?" she says abruptly.

"Oh, sorry." I change the subject. "How did you get involved in the agency? Did you work for one in the States?"

"No, just fell into it." She digs into her stew.

She shuts me down even faster when I ask why my paychecks are so small. She's hiding something. She's a tough girl, scarred from I don't know what. I can tell she doesn't have a formal education. It's so confusing because I really like her, but I can't trust her. Moreover, her promiscuity makes me nervous and triggers my own issues and traumas around sex.

One night we go out to dinner and to see Robert Palmer in concert. She brings a date so there are three of us. She wears a red minidress under a black leather biker jacket with fishnets held up with a garter belt and red spike heels. Oh, and no panties. As the wine goes down, she reminds us for the second time that she's pantyless and guides her date's hand under her dress. I sit opposite them in the small booth, kind of stimulated, but even more nervous. They start making out, while he fondles her pussy.

Yes, it's hot, and if I were more in charge of my own body, and decisions around sexuality, maybe I could have chosen to enjoy this moment. Maybe even join in—or not join in. As I look back, it would have been nice to be free to make that choice, rather than chained to my strict code of sex, the rules of which I didn't even know.

✦

Scarlett has been working primarily in Germany, and we haven't gone out to dinner together in way too long. We decide to go to Le Refuge des Fondus in Montmartre, famous for its fondue and red wine served in baby bottles.

Multicolored graffiti covers every surface of the tiny restaurant. French jazz fills the grimy, happy room. A singing waiter with a thick brown mustache helps me onto and over the table to the bench on the other side. Another brings us old-fashioned French baby bottles, filled with red wine and topped with rubber nipples. Sucking on a glass baby bottle is embarrassing at first, but after half a bottle, I feel like all wine should be drunk like this.

A group of American college girls enters the restaurant, immediately pissing me off because college students in Paris are spoiled brats living a cushy life on their parents' bank accounts. Yes, I'm jealous.

They end up being so nice and so much fun that they break down my foolish preconceived opinions. Soon we're all dipping bread and sausages in the melted cheese, talking, and screaming in laughter. They mention that a room in their apartment is up for rent. I had wanted an apartment for months but was too afraid to commit to that financially. This one is so reasonable that we jump at the chance. Scarlett and I move in.

Our new home, number 76 Boulevard Magenta, is a five-story

Haussmann building built around 1850, elegant and filthy with limestone walls, a zinc roof, and ornate iron balconies. It faces the wide boulevard with speeding cars and is close to the Gare du Nord train station. No tight-woven streets full of tourists like our hotel homes in Saint-Germain.

A skeleton key opens the massive wood courtyard door and another opens our apartment on the fourth floor (American fifth floor, no elevator, of course). The teeny kitchen is next to the landlord's bedroom, which she has set up in the apartment's original living room. Layers of dirty white paint cover the wood and plasterwork. There is a beautiful yet dirty marble fireplace with an antique trumeau mirror hung above it. She's got a small TV on a rolling tray and her bed is in the middle of the room.

A bath at the end of the hall has a pistachio-green sink and miniature tub. One bedroom is divided in two, so the landlord can rent both sides. Selim, a Turkish man, lives on one side, and my new friend Ruby would soon move into the other. Down the hall is the bedroom where the American college girls sleep. Scarlett's and my room is opposite theirs and has tall windows that open to the sky above and courtyard below.

French oak floors laid in a herringbone pattern are deteriorating gracefully on the floor. Faded red geometric wallpaper peels from the walls and a beat-up sofa sits under the windows. A wood rod works well as our closet, and next to the bedroom door is a small card table for our supplies: peanut butter, Swiss army knife, two electric coils to boil water, and two mugs. A tiny room in the corner holds a miniature sink and toilet, and we sleep in child-size French twins with soft, faded turquoise sheets. I'm thrilled to be out of the hotels.

Madame, as my landlord likes to be called, is from Vietnam. Her sweet, humble smile lights up a room. She's fortyish and nowhere near five feet tall. Her floral cotton dresses are always covered with bulky sweaters and an apron. Magnifying glasses hang from a chain around her neck.

Her thick Vietnamese accent causes choppiness in her French, which I think is adorable. Because she's a seamstress, we bond easily and enjoy our evenings hanging out in the tiny, simple kitchen, cooking and laughing. I make *salade vert* with Dijon dressing, while she makes homemade tofu with cinnamon and sugar. The two of us can finish off a whole potful.

Madame and her family had fled the Vietnam War in the sixties for safety in Paris. Yet, one terrible morning she woke to an empty house, with her husband and children gone. He had taken them back to Vietnam. She must have felt totally helpless—I never had the nerve to ask why she didn't follow. She stayed in Paris with a broken heart, yearning for her children. After we became friends, I think she was afraid I would leave her too. I could tell because it took her a long time to open up to me. She wanted to be sure I was a permanent fixture, not just a renter passing through.

On my first night in Madame's, I dream completely in French. The next morning, I am totally switched to thinking in French—even when I'm awake. It is effortless and natural. I no longer think in English and I love it. This apartment feels like a real home, private, like my own secret world, off-limits to anyone, especially non-French-speaking people. I finally bond with so many people I live among in this city. We know we have something in common, our own language. I'm a member of an exclusive, private club. A French club.

Finally a page in Vogue Paris!

REVOLVING DOOR OF MODELS

May to June 1980

Just as I'm reaching my stride personally, Scarlett leaves Paris to work in Milan. Living with her makes me feel safe, and even though we're different, she's a good friend and I love her. We always laugh at our crazy circumstances together and share our trials and triumphs. I miss her terribly and am shocked as I realize how much I depended on her emotionally.

A model's life can be lonely, and relationships difficult. Constant travel makes it hard to build trust and nurture friendships. It seems like right when I meet a girl I like, she leaves town unannounced. I never find out if she's given up and gone home or what. Some models only come to town to do the couture shows. They're the nearly six-foot-tall beauties who rule the runway. Then there are the "perfect" ones who come for magazine shoots and fly back to New York. There aren't many like me who just stick around, stubbornly trying to make it. I have funny memories of crazy, drunken dinners with other models that end in smashing plates on the floor and of the time a model flung a huge clump of whipped cream onto a biker dude's black leather jacket—he didn't think it was funny though.

After Scarlett leaves, a male flight attendant for Air France becomes my closest friend. Alain holds parties at his apartment, where we models cook meals from our native countries. Bitten, from Denmark, makes meatballs with boiled potatoes; and Anna, from Sweden, makes crepes with lingonberry jam and whipped cream. After dinner we all stroll together in the Latin Quarter, entertained by street musicians, fire-eaters, knife swallowers, and mimes. Still, it is hard to coordinate time together with all of us traveling so much. Mostly, I am alone.

Finally, Ruby, a new American girl from Atlanta, moves in, sharing the other side of Selim's room that Madame divided in two. Ruby's wavy red hair and big breasts are unusual for a model. I hope we can become close friends, but it's not long before she moves in with an English photographer. Meanwhile, my room with the extra twin bed is a revolving door of girls. Most steal my clothes, skip out on rent, sleep their way to magazine editorial, and leave. Each one reminds me that the traditional way to the top in this business is to use your body for more than modeling.

Since I'm a permanent fixture at Paris Planning, the agents seem totally comfortable conducting their crazy deals right in front of me. They offer me a job to shoot swimwear in the Caribbean or Africa, and I think, *Hell yes*, until they tell me that I'm expected to have sex with the photographer. When I refuse, they pick up the phone and offer the job to another model. This happens so many times, and it kills me to pass up beautiful location shoots. I know the pictures will be amazing and the location will feel like a holiday, and I want to go so bad! I wish I could bring myself to do it. But I can't. I don't know how I got this moral code. I don't even understand my moral code. I think it's not about selling out. I want to achieve my successes honestly, without using my body for sexual manipulation. I want to feel like I deserve what I accomplish. Not like I cheated my way in.

As the months roll by, when new girls come to town, I don't warn them anymore about the agency's tricks and traps. I now look at it as part of the game. I figure each girl deserves to make her own choices, and it's none of my business what they decide to do. I've changed, become colder about the business, and somewhat detached. I don't trust anyone at the agency anymore. Now I'm a pro at using the agency for what they're good at and ignoring the bullshit. Although Gerald continues to give me the cold shoulder, I manage to work solid all through May, June, and July. Even though I only take home a fraction of the money I make, my bank account is growing and I continue to spend carefully and save.

I'm collecting new magazine tear sheets every week from *Cosmo*, *20ans*, plus many more. And I finally have two full pages in *Vogue Paris*. My face is plastered on bus stops and Metro tunnels. My portfolio is full of great test photographers' work, and I did it all without sleeping with photographers. It just took a hell of a lot longer.

There are always a select few girls who don't have to deal with these games. They fit into the top one percent of models and are treated totally different from the rest of us. They are lucky girls who have won the genetic jackpot and have the perfect combination of attributes that are "hot" right now. (What is hot changes constantly.) Things they usually have in common are: long hair, straight white teeth, big eyes, small noses, lips that are full on top and bottom, faces with baby fat, thin hips, perfect skin, and tall, lanky bodies.

They also seem to be less dysfunctional than some of the other girls. They reek of confidence and look like they don't give a shit about modeling. It seems to make the client feel lucky to be using them. They're the agency's "stars." Gerald books them instantly for *Vogue* and *Elle* editorial. They work with the best hair and makeup artists, stylists, and photographers. They get all the cosmetics and designer campaigns and earn the most money. They are never sent to parties or asked to sleep with photographers. I'm obviously not a part of this group.

Me, a lovely man, and his camel in Tunisia, 1980

THE CAMEL

June 1980, Tunisia

Paris is having a false spring, which is basically no spring. There definitely hasn't been any sign of summer this year. Being from California, it's hard not to let the darkness affect me. But when it really starts pulling me down, I seem to land a shoot in the sun.

On June fifteenth, I board a flight from Paris in freezing, dark drizzle. As the plane ascends through thick clouds, the cabin instantly fills with light. The sunny baby blue sky has been above me the whole time, blinded by heavy gray clouds. Light, warmth, and joy radiate into me.

Tunisia, North Africa, is across the Mediterranean from Sicily, Italy. I have never seen a landscape like it—all white sand and turquoise waters. (Back home the sand is brown and the water green.) The buildings are bright white plaster domes and arches. I jump on a rickety bus at the airport with standing room only. We all grab a rope loop overhead and hang on.

Friendly, dark-skinned locals are crammed in tight. Old men smoke non-filters through missing teeth. They're gorgeous to me. A cloud of black smoke engulfs the bus as the driver steps on the gas. Every time we hit a pothole on the sandy road, all of us catapult into the air. With each pothole, we laugh harder. The scene outside the glassless windows is so beautiful I can't believe it's real: Women wrapped in brightly colored fabrics carry baskets of fruit on their heads and walk along with their children. I love this place already.

I meet Sylvie, the owner of Rasurel Swimwear, in the lobby of the Djerba Menzel hotel. She tells me to go lie by the pool to get some color. I have never sunbathed topless, but as I look around, no one is staring at my boobs. It's nice not fussing around with a bikini top and tan lines.

The intense African sun soaks my bones, and the pool is so quiet I hear my own breath. I close my eyes and soon fall asleep. I don't know how much time has passed, but when I sit up, blood rushes to my head with a bang. I get up slowly, walk dizzily to my room, and look in the bathroom mirror. My skin is already dark red, not Parisian pale—closer, I think, to my California color, but I'm not sure because it's been so long since I've been tan.

I get the urge to cut my hair. I can hear Willy say, "Grow your hair long—no bangs!" I ignore her and take the nail scissors from my toiletry bag. I'm taking control of my life a few hairs at a time.

In the evening, glowing lanterns light the winding path to the restaurant. The room is draped in bright pink, turquoise, and purple silk. Sylvie, Henri, the photographer, and I sit on pillows around a low brass table. A handsome man in a turban and caftan holds a brass bowl and kettle for us to wash our hands, as we will use them, not silverware. We scoop spiced fish, vegetables, and couscous onto soft, warm pita bread. Dessert is baklava with crusty layers of honey and cinnamon. The client, Sylvie, never notices I cut my hair.

By the end of dinner, I'm not feeling so good. I don't tell them I'm nauseous and about to faint. I try to act normal. On the way to my room, dizziness and nausea take over. My head throbs, then my skin ignites. I strip my clothes off and look in the mirror. I've never been this color before. I hurry to collapse on the bed before I faint. I try not to move while my body flashes from shivering to sizzling and burning. The sheets are thorns, my head spins, and I worry about the shoot tomorrow. I listen to Arabic radio all night long.

Waking up disoriented is normal—those first few moments when I scan the room for clues that hint at which country I'm in. Today though, my burning skin tells me I'm in Tunisia. I tiptoe to the bathroom to look at the damage and, thankfully, it doesn't look as bad as it feels. I throw on a loose T-shirt, but no underwear because panty creases are not allowed in swim shots, to meet Sylvie and Henri for breakfast.

A sandy trail leads to a deserted beach, where transparent turquoise waves pound the pale sand. I change under a towel held together by Sylvie's fingertips. These suits were obviously fitted on French girls, with their tiny hips, unlike me with the curves. They hurt as I pull them over my hips.

I love working with these clients. They're calm and respectful—no drama. After shooting all morning, I'm stunned when a man walks up the beach with his camel. I had never seen anything this exotic. He lets me pet the camel, and when I look into the old man's eyes, he feels utterly familiar to me. Have you ever met someone randomly and, when your eyes meet, the entire space around you becomes totally focused on the connection between the two of you? Like you already know them somehow? Well, that happens with the man with the camel.

We go sightseeing in Tunis, shopping in souks and eating couscous and fish outdoors in the square. Tunis is a beautiful and friendly city and I love being here. I forget about the daily grind of go-sees and pretend for a few days that I have a normal working life. Surrounded by nature and respect, I grow more peaceful each day.

Ten days in Tunisia rejuvenates my spirit, and when I return to Paris I land the cover of *Olympe*, the French version of American *Self*.

Chasing the photographer Georges Vidon's
car through the French countryside

CALIFORNIA SUCKS

August 1980

The only connection I have to my old life in California are rare phone calls and the letters I receive. I check my mailbox in the agency hoping for a letter.

A card from Mom brings me up to speed on her Yorkies, while Dad writes about the fire station and the vintage car he's working on. My friend Penny and I write back and forth every few weeks. She tells me about college and her boyfriend, and I vent to her about modeling. In her latest letter, she asks me to be a bridesmaid in her wedding in November. My old boyfriend Jack's letters are full of pleas to come home, saying he wants to marry me. He even draws wedding rings in the margins. I left him at the gate at LAX, hoping for a big distance that would end our sick relationship. But he still isn't buying the fact that we're broken up.

Alleen writes, saying she is skipping her annual design trip to Paris and could I do the research for her? Of course I can. I shop all the swimwear lines in the city and carefully choose suits with ideas that will translate successfully into the US market. I try them all on, pin them, and attach notes on how to alter them.

I send fabric samples with treatments we don't have the technology for in America, like iron-on rhinestones and metallic foil printing. I pack the swimsuits, magazines, sketches, and my design report all together and ship it off to Alleen in California. It's exhilarating to have this kind of challenge and use my design skills and creativity again. I almost forgot I have them.

August is dead in Paris because everyone goes on vacation. I impulsively decide to visit family and friends in California. I buy a plane ticket and leave without really thinking the whole thing through. I have no idea it will be the beginning of a downward spiral. Time in Paris has changed me, but I'm not aware how much until I'm back in Downey.

Dad picks me up at the Air France terminal at LAX in his Mustang Boss 302 and opens it up on the 405 Freeway. "Whoa, Dad, it feels like we're going a hundred and twenty!"

"No, Jillie, we're only going a hundred." He laughs.

That night, at a party at Jack's, I learn one of my friends is sleeping with him. I shouldn't care, but I didn't think friends should sleep with other friends' ex-boyfriends.

During the week, I check in at Wilhelmina. "Jill! What are you doing here? We thought you were never coming back."

"I'm not back, I just came to say hi."

"Well, look what Paris has done to you!" Steve, my agent, says.

After a short visit, I ask to see the agency head alone in her office. After taking a deep breath, I say, "You know what goes on in Paris, right? All the parties?"

"What are you talking about?" she asks.

"Seriously. You don't know? They make us go to parties, and if we don't go, they don't give us interviews. Oh, and they take seventy percent of our money. They say it's for taxes, but I don't believe it."

She shakes her head. "Paris Planning is the top agency in Paris. I've never heard of any of this." I am clearly wasting my time and feel stupid for even bringing it up. I decide to leave and go vintage shopping on Melrose and over to Tower Records on Sunset instead.

I feel like an outsider everywhere I go. Everyone's lives have gone on without me. Plus, I have a bad case of jet lag and my first menstrual period in six months. I can't sleep. My boobs, stomach, and back all ache. I stay in bed feeling shitty. Why did I come?

I feel claustrophobic in my parents' house. I miss the streets of Paris, the cafés, and the guy at the crepe cart across from the agency. I miss speaking in French. The French language sounds like a song, pretty and romantic, light and airy. It makes me feel sophisticated, worldly. English feels clunky now, too blunt, serious, and choppy. I don't like it. I miss my shabby little room with the faded turquoise sheets. I miss Paris. I throw my concert T-shirts, the used men's tuxedo shirt and bow tie I bought on Melrose, and my new red-and-black lizard cowboy boots in my suitcase and count the hours to departure.

I get back to Paris on Friday night, with the banks closed till Monday. I have fifteen francs—fewer than four dollars—and it has to last all weekend. There's not a crumb of food on my card table, not even peanut butter. I go to bed hungry.

Saturday morning I buy a large packet of Knorr's powdered soup to spread out over two days. I feel like I'm starving. My stomach churns, and when I can't stand it anymore, I make a tiny cup of watery soup. I would never impose on Madame to ask for food.

With my body clock messed up, I sleep all day and flop around anxiously all night. I'm shattered, confused, sad, and sleep deprived. I cry on and off but can't figure out why. My only sanity is the music that plays through the headphones of my Walkman.

Why did I want to go to California anyway? What a waste of energy, the strangest trip ever. I feel like I've been shot into space in a rocket, spun around, and thrown down in a splat onto the ground. I'm so lost. Where is home? Is Paris home? What the hell am I doing with my life?

◆

On Monday morning, I hit the bank and get breakfast. I have a go-see for a two-week lingerie job in Paris. My breasts are swollen from having my period in California, so all the bras and everything else fit perfectly. The following week, when it's time to shoot, my breasts have deflated and the bras are a little loose. The client throws a huge tantrum, yelling at me in front of the entire crew. I feel like a failure. Heavy shame and humiliation envelop me because of my small breasts.

Every time I go to change in the dressing room, I breathe fast and I fight back tears. In front of the camera, I hold my breath, trying to fill out the bras, and worry the camera will pick up on my sadness. I'm in a mental pit.

After a marathon nine-day shoot, it's finally over. My back is sore and stiff from holding lingerie poses. The sky is cloudy, gray, and almost dark as I walk away from the studio. I can finally let my guard down.

Crossing a cobblestone bridge on the way to the bus stop, something hits me and I feel totally disoriented. I hear the client's comments about my breasts repeating over and over in my mind, and I become overwhelmed with self-hatred and guilt. I flash to Dad's porno wall, him saying, "Her tits are the perfect shape and size, Jillie." But mine aren't and everybody's upset about it. Why is my breast size so fucking important? But it is. These jobs pay my rent.

I sit in the back of the bus, hiding my tears, detached, catatonic, staring out the window all the way to Magenta. I get off and walk slowly down my street, saying hello to the prostitutes I see every single day. They always make me sad. I watch as they negotiate a price and get in a car. They'll be back to their post, their doorway, soon enough, standing, smoking, waiting for the next job. But how is modeling any different? We rent our bodies out by the hour. I wonder what their hourly rate is compared to mine?

I wind up the five flights of stairs, pull my clothes off, and climb in bed. I reach for the Bible my friend's parents gave me. I never got past the genealogies so I use it as a journal, writing in the back margins. I grab a pen and write to God, who I don't know. I write that I'll do any kind of work. It doesn't have to be modeling. I'll work in a sawmill if that's what I'm supposed to do. I don't care. I'm tired of fighting. I need a new focus, one that's good for me. I can't take the fog that has come over me. I hear a voice that says, "Love the people of Paris." I take it to heart.

In the days after hearing that message, I try to spread a little love around as I go about town doing my business—simple things like helping older people. I try to connect with some of Paris's elderly, more callous people. After all, they have lived through World War II, Nazi occupation, and a decade of postwar poverty. They aren't friendly like Madame or the young waiters at my favorite café. They are cold and hardened by a difficult life.

When I go into a nice boutique, and the elderly saleslady sneers at me, I smile warmly to her. To my absolute shock, she smiles back. I feel love flow through me. I do it on the bus, on the street, and with homeless people.

One day on the Metro, I hear "Get off at Madeleine" from somewhere inside and figure, why not? So, I get off at Madeleine, and at the bottom of the stairs is a tiny, hunchbacked old lady crouched next to a huge box, crowds of people whizzing past. No one stops to ask if she needs help. I approach and ask timidly if I can help her. She nods, still hunched over, saying, "Oui, oui, s'il vous plaît."

I help carry the heavy box up the stairs and set it down. I go back down to help her out of the Metro, and then take her and her box to a taxi stand and hail a cab. She is so grateful, holding on to my hands, shaking them in the street. My heart swells. This is a hell of a lot more fun than seeing myself in a magazine. And, finally, the darkness that started on my trip to California begins to lift.

✦

Early one morning, I go out walking. It's still dark and the city isn't awake. I wander all the way to the financial district, and as I come around a corner, I spy a freshly delivered, cellophane-wrapped pallet of magazines by a newsstand. I wonder if my new *Olympe* cover is in there. Checking to make sure no one's looking, I rip a hole in the top and dig down into the heap. Halfway down, I find *Olympe* magazine with me on the cover and pull it out. It's a good, strong cover, just what I need. This will finally open the door to better magazines.

I stand there feeling certain that the success I've been chasing is actually attainable. Then, seconds later, I'm suddenly confused. I don't know if I want it anymore. My mind races with multiple scenarios where Paris Planning and Wilhelmina are totally running my life and I have no control. I'll be working nonstop, booked on back-to-back shoots all over the world, with no personal life at all. No time for peaceful reflection, just racing around, airport to airport.

I don't want to be owned by them, and I don't want to be chained to this business. I'm not instantly fulfilled. Instead I feel hollow, like a deep, dirty pit. This feels like a whole new set of problems. I already know what modeling is, and there's so much ugliness and lies. Do I really want to devote my life to it?

Now I fly under the agency's radar, in control of my plans. But success will hijack me and run me into the ground. I already know I'm not good at saying no. My freedom will dissolve and I'll lose myself, and my barely stable footing. I don't have a very good hold on myself to begin with.

Right then I get the urgent desire to travel far away, where no one knows me. I want to get lost in a foreign city. After exercising my muscles of adaptability, I now crave the unfamiliar. I want to be lost again. I want to be uncomfortable and alone so I can hear my inner voice, somewhere I don't speak the language. Maybe Japan. I could get lost in Japan. I need to get the fuck out of here.

Silica sand quarry, Fontainebleau, France, 1980

MONTE CARLO

August 24, 1980, Paris and Monaco

I sit in my little bed, writing a list of places I could go: Italy, Japan, Germany. Maybe a long vacation on a beach, where I can get my head straight. I have plenty of money right now, and the job I just finished paid double because it was lingerie. As I write my list of sunny vacation spots, the phone rings.

"Gilles! *Le téléphone est pour vous!*" Madame yells down the hallway.

I run to her room, to the phone on the marble fireplace. "*Oui, âllo?*"

"Jill, it's Pepper. What are you doing?"

"Just hanging out."

"I'm calling to see if you'd like to come to Monte Carlo with me this weekend."

"That's crazy, I was sitting here trying to think of where to go for vacation. Isn't Monte Carlo superexpensive though?"

"Oh, this trip's free. You don't have to pay for anything."

"I've heard that before. You're kidding, right?" Finally I say, "Nothing's free, little Poivre, but I'll bring a lot of cash and I can run fast. I'm in!"

"Great, I'll arrange everything and pick you up Friday after work."

Pepper and I fly into Nice and drive along the coastal cliffs and seaside beaches. I absorb the glistening Mediterranean. The beach at Cannes is peppered with topless sunbathers. Ladies confidently basking with boobs hanging to their waists make me smile.

Driving into Monte Carlo, you could almost smell the money. Manicured gardens filled with red, purple, and yellow flowers surround elaborate, sparkling fountains, and jewelry and couture stores seem to be everywhere. Grand palaces with ornate facades wave international flags. It looks like a miniature Paris on the sea—except bright, sunny, and much cleaner.

We pull into the grand entrance of the Loews Hotel, where an army of doormen and valets in suits and top hats greet us. (I have no idea that one day I would stay at this very hotel every year for the International Swimwear Convention in Monte Carlo.) The massive lobby's polished marble floors reflect the bright sunlight. A piano bar overlooking the sea has floor-to-ceiling glass. As I stand looking out, the sea sparkles all the way to the horizon.

We take the elevator to our sunny room, with its own balcony and view of the sea. The butter yellow–striped wallpaper, floral bedding, and white faux bamboo furniture give it a happy vibe. As we settle in, Pepper suggests I go for a massage. It would be my first time, but why not?

I make my way downstairs to the spa desk, where a woman signs me in and directs me to the locker room. I take everything off except my silky green panties and put on a white robe. I go to the massage room, put the robe on a hook, and lie on the table under a white sheet. A skinny French man comes in and rubs oil on his hands. He pulls the sheet aside and begins massaging my legs fast and not gently. I try and relax.

He then shoves his hand up between my thighs. I jam my legs together while he fights to get into my panties, moaning. I flip a switch and my adrenaline kicks in. I grab the sheet and run to the dressing room. I pull my clothes from the locker, then race to the elevator and all the way back to our room still wrapped in the sheet, heart beating fast, focused on getting to safety. I throw on my bikini bottom and a T-shirt and go to the pool, looking for Pepper. I spot her on a lounge and rush over.

"Pepper, the massage guy stuck his hand up my vagina!" I'm breathing fast.

"What are you talking about? The masseur?"

"Yes, that creepy masseur!"

She bolts from her cushion. "I'm calling the desk." She returns a few minutes later, laughing. "I called the spa, and the lady who answered is the masseur's wife! He's busted."

But I don't find it funny. I am still shaken up. "You look like you need a drink," Pepper says.

"Good idea." I take a deep breath.

"Monsieur, we'd like something to drink, please," Pepper sings in French. She is over my episode. The waiter hands us a menu with color photos of drinks topped with flowers and umbrellas.

"*Une* yellow polka-dot bikini, *s'il vous plaît*," I say.

"*Moi aussi*," Pepper agrees.

He returns with two pastel yellow drinks topped with whipped cream and purple orchids. I have no idea what is in them, but I have at least two. Pepper's friends join us at the pool: Andrew and his preppy sister, Giada, who seem like rich college kids from the East Coast. They are on break from school in Switzerland and visiting their dad in Monaco. Lucky them. All of us Americans bake in the warm sun, laughing, showing off our French to one another. The polka-dot bikinis do the trick, and I am finally relaxed and a little drunk.

"Gilles, we've been invited to a party tonight in Cannes. Gotta be ready by eight. You wanna take a nap?"

"That sounds perfect," I say.

We close the curtains and pass out until the front desk calls at 7:30 P.M.

"Did you bring a dress?" Pepper asks.

"No, I've got a skirt and a men's tuxedo shirt from the forties."

"I'm wearing this." She holds up a tight black dress. "I've got to get alone with Andrew. Isn't he gorgeous?" She puts her leg on the bed, pulling up her stockings and attaching them to her garter belt.

"Don't you think he's a little young for you?" I ask.

"He's not too young. He's in college."

"He's too young for me and you're older than me. What is he, like eighteen?" I tie my bow tie. "You're crazy, Poivre."

After a knock, Pepper runs to open the door. Andrew is standing there, seriously handsome—the spitting image of John F. Kennedy Jr. He looks perfectly comfortable in a suit. The only time I see guys in suits at home are at proms and weddings. I feel instantly intimidated, telling myself I am too old for him, which is just an excuse I make up in my head. In reality, I don't feel good enough. Andrew is a sophisticated, white-collar college kid. Me? I'm blue-collar, not in college, a model.

"Hi, baby!" Pepper purrs.

"Hey, girls, my dad's downstairs with the car, are you ready?"

"I'm ready." I watch him out of the corner of my eye because he's so handsome, while Pepper's hot on his trail.

We find his dad, Dominic, and sister, Giada, waiting in the lobby. I can see where he gets his good looks. Dominic is handsome, with dark olive skin and thick salt-and-pepper hair. He looks Greek or Italian. His shirt is unbuttoned partway, showing his chest. Giada looks like a young version of Jackie O. *How do they even look like this?* I wonder.

"So this is the famous Gilles I've been hearing about. You're just as beautiful as Pepper said. I'm so glad to meet such a lovely young lady."

"Thanks, nice to meet you too. Dominic, right?"

"Yes, and this is my daughter, Giada. And you obviously know Andrew."

"Yes, we all met at the pool."

"Ladies, gentleman, shall we?" Dominic holds his arm out, leading us to the black Rolls-Royce limousine.

"This car reminds me of an old Jaguar limo my dad fixed up. It had a little bar in the back like this."

"So your dad's a car buff?" Dominic asks.

I nod. "A big car buff."

"I love cars too." Dominic pops a bottle of Cristal as we drive through Monaco. The grand palaces, Casino de Monte-Carlo, Casino Café de Paris, and the beautiful Hôtel de Paris are spectacular at night. I don't think Monte Carlo has a bad section. All this wealth makes me feel safer somehow. I think about Grace Kelly, Princess of Monaco, who married the wealthy prince. "Hey, girls, should we go gambling after dinner? Did you bring your passports?" he asks.

"Jill's not old enough. You know the law, you have to be twenty-one," Pepper says.

"Can't I sneak in?" I want to see the inside of these beautiful old buildings.

"No way. Trust me, you don't want to get in trouble here. They take their gambling laws very seriously," Dominic says.

We speed down the winding coast, drinking champagne and singing along to music all the way to Cannes.

Earth crunches under the tires as we pull off the cliffside highway and roll to a stop. "We're here!" Dominic shouts. We pile out and wander in the dark instinctively toward the music, twinkling lights, and huge fire in the distance.

"What is this place?" I ask. Pepper body-slams me, wrapping her arms around my chest, singing "La Vie en Rose" in drunken French. I wobble in my black suede pumps through the dirt.

Dominic puts his hand around my waist. "Jill, this is the famous old Le Pirate, come on, you'll see!"

The music intensifies as we get closer. I can't believe my eyes— I see hordes of long-haired, tattooed, shirtless pirates, strumming guitars and banging tambourines. A crackling bonfire blazes twenty feet high, lighting up the dark night. I look overhead, where more pirates are climbing on ropes with daggers clinched between their teeth. It is like a scene out of *Pirates of the Caribbean*, except the movie hasn't been made yet.

A long table sparkles with candles, crystal, and silver, and at the head sits a young Egyptian-looking girl with dark exotic eyes and jet-black hair. Her beaded dress shimmers in the flickering light. Sophisticated ladies and gentlemen converse animatedly around the table.

In the past, I may have felt out of place, but after modeling in Paris, I can fit in anywhere. Suddenly, a suited man stands up and hurls his champagne glass into the fire. Another guy throws his on the rocks and shards of glass fly. Adrenaline rushes through me as pandemonium breaks out. Of course, I jump right in. "I love this place!" I scream to Pepper. "It's better than the Greek restaurants in Saint-Germain!"

"I bet Hollywood doesn't have places like this, does it?" she yells back.

A dark-tanned, greasy old pirate hands us each a glass of champagne. "*Salut!*" I take a swig while another pirate pulls out my chair. Dominic begins introducing the other guests at the table, which was futile with the thundering music. I shake hands, nod, and smile anyway.

Plates of baked potatoes with sour cream and caviar are served. I pucker at the salty, fishy taste. I gulp champagne and hurl my glass in the fire. A pirate promptly brings me another. As the Spanish guitars, tambourines, and drums speed up I want to dance, not eat, so I stand up and throw my plate of food in the fire.

As I turn back around, I notice a man smiling, watching me, smiling and laughing a little. Normally, this would be creepy, but it's not. He reminds me of my friend's dad, whom I danced with at a wedding. I smile and sit down. As he brings his chair over next to mine, I'm glad he isn't some young guy who's going to try to sleep with me. His short stature, round tummy, and balding head give me the upper hand. I feel in control of the situation.

It is too loud to talk, so he takes my hands and pulls me up to dance, and we twirl together all around the dusty ground. It feels as if we'd already danced together many years before. The pirates gather around and the guests clap with the music. Suddenly, he stops, grabs a chair, and throws it into the fire. Flames envelop the chair, turning it to a charred skeleton. He's laughing, and I hurl one in too. Then we laugh at each other and slam together again like two magnets, whirling around to the gypsy music in front of the flames.

It is only us dancing. Everyone else is drinking and laughing at the festive table, making a pretty backdrop for our world. Musicians circle us again, and he and a pirate grab my hands and feet, scoop me up, and swing me back and forth like a rag doll. I let my head fall back with my hair grazing the dirt, watching the flames upside down. I am totally surrendered to the spirit of the party, euphoric with freedom.

They lower me to the ground, and I stagger slightly to the table. My new friend helps me into my chair but he remains standing, watching me. When he lowers himself slowly onto his chair, he leans toward my face, his sparkling eyes locked on mine. We sit looking at each other and start laughing again. Then he tenderly pulls my left arm, palm up, onto the table, pushes my sleeve up, and writes *I love you*, in blood, down my forearm. It takes me a minute to realize it's blood. I'm stunned, but I like it. It feels like we've made some kind of secret pact.

A pirate sees the blood and whisks him away for a bandage.

Time stands still, and all I can do is look at the bright red words. All the noise falls silent in the middle of the madness. My heart soars overhead like a bird. I keep the blood on my arm.

Pepper rushes over. "Let me see your arm. Are you bleeding?" As the words register, she screams, "Oh my God, Jill. It says *I love you*! Do you know who that was?"

Her words, like a slap in the face, pull me out of my dream state. "No. How would I know?"

"It's Adnan Khashoggi," she screams into my ear.

"I can't hear you. Tell me later!" I plea.

Pepper knows her way around a party, and realizes I'm drunk. She takes my hand and the two of us walk to the rocky cliff and sit on a boulder overlooking the water. It is suddenly much quieter. I feel the cool, salty breeze pass over my face as we stare at the glistening sea below, and the boat lights twinkling in the distance. It is one of those nights where the moon reflects on the water like a sparkling road coming straight at you.

My head starts spinning. This is not good. Pepper sees the look on my face and sneaks behind me, putting her arms around me in the Heimlich maneuver and squeezes hard. I throw up all over the rocks. "Why did you do that?" I gag.

"You'll thank me in the morning," Pepper says in her tough girl, street-smart way. "I lived with an alcoholic and did that to him all the time. Are you okay? I'm gonna go talk to Dominic." She leaves me on the rock.

Eventually, the party dwindles down. The music slows and people head to their cars. I am drained. Pepper and Dominic come over to me. Pepper leans in close and whispers, "Adnan wants you to come have coffee with him on his boat."

"Who?" I still couldn't understand the name she said.

"The man you were dancing with."

"Oh, thank you, no, I'm tired. I just want to go to bed," I say.

They look at each other and whisper back and forth. Finally, Dominic says, "Jill, do you see that ship way out there? That's his."

It looks like the *Queen Mary* all lit up in the night. My mouth tastes like vomit, and my head is spinning. I can't imagine going on a ship right now, no matter how big it is. "Not tonight." Coffee? Sure he wants coffee.

We pile into the limo and drive back to the hotel. I sit between a blond-haired girl in a blue dress and Pepper. I sway side to side with the curves in the road as the girl in the blue dress whines at me to stop leaning on her.

The next morning, Pepper orders breakfast from room service. Time to get up. I drag myself out of bed and onto the balcony. The morning sea is totally still. It's already warm, and the sun makes my head pound. Then a splash of dark red catches my eye. My arm is covered in dried blood. Last night's party rushes back, and I laugh to myself.

Pepper is bubbly and way too awake. "What a party! Wasn't that great?" She giggles. "Aren't you glad I made you throw up?"

I am not ready for this. "Yeah, it was crazy, and yes, thank you for that." I am still coming to.

"After I dropped you off, I went to Andrew's room." She smirks, lighting a cigarette.

"You're crazy. He's a baby, Pepper."

"Not last night."

There's a welcome knock at the door and Pepper answers it. The hotel waiter has brought a silver platter overflowing with goodies—and thank God, two cafés au lait. He sets the tray down on the balcony.

Pepper keeps babbling on excitedly. I think it's sex euphoria.

After breakfast, I get back in bed and stare out at the sea. Dominic calls around noon.

"Yes, great! See you later," Pepper says in French, and hangs up the phone, gleaming. "Jill, you're invited to Adnan's yacht for dinner tonight. He really wants to see you."

"Who?" I want to be sure we are talking about the same person.

"Adnan, the man you were dancing with last night—the one with the blood? He wants you to come to his boat for dinner," she says.

I thought about the night before. It was totally crazy and fun. I don't know if it was my artistic nature or the adrenaline junkie in me, but I liked the blood. I found it romantic. I wanted to see him out of curiosity, but I was also nervous. Who writes in blood and owns a big ship like that? "Okay, I'll go, but only if you come with me," I finally say.

"Of course I'll come!"

We relax at the pool without the fancy drinks this time. The sun and sea bring back memories of childhood vacations on the water, so I pretend that I am in California. With my imagination, I can teleport myself anywhere.

Around 4 P.M. we go upstairs to get ready. I have only a small bag of clothes, so I pull on a white eyelet skirt and wrap an orange scarf around my chest as a top. I wear my white moccasins—perfect deck shoes.

Fontainebleau, France, 1980

ABOARD THE *NABILA*

Pepper and I meet Dominic at the dock in Cannes, triple-cheek kiss, and jump into a speedboat. The sea breeze is cool on my face as we bounce through the gentle waves. It feels like home.

Adnan's ship is too large for the harbor, so it is anchored way out. The huge vessel towers four stories overhead and stretches over a hundred feet in each direction. We pull up to a floating dock, wood slats bobbing and slapping the water. I instinctively jump onto the dock and grab the chrome rail of the speedboat, pulling it to the dock. I hold a hand out to catch the rope from the boat driver.

The sound of the plastic bumpers squeaking between the dock and the boat is so familiar. I hold the boat while Pepper and Dominic disembark. The crew is surprised by my moves. A narrow wood stairway with aluminum handrails descends from the ship. We climb up to the mid-deck, where Adnan greets us.

He gives me a huge hug and kisses on my cheeks. "Gilles! How are you? Did you have a good sleep? I missed you." Then he gets right to the point. "Why didn't you come for coffee?"

"I was too tired." I smile. "That was so much fun. Especially the bonfire—I didn't know I was so destructive."

I am finally able to get a good look. He is shorter than me, about five-five. His head is round and balding on top. His skin is tanned olive, and he has a mustache, long dark eyelashes, brown eyes, and an adorable smile. He has a round belly and is impeccably dressed. And clean. I always notice clean. He smells good. There is something about his eyes. He looks like a happy person. He has more than a trace of an accent.

"So, where are you from?" I ask.

"I'm from Saudi Arabia. Well, my family is Turkish and Syrian, but I was born in Mecca in Saudi Arabia." His voice is calm, confident, and has an upbeat ring to it.

"Oh, I was trying to figure out your accent. You remind me of my favorite neighbors I grew up with in California. They were from Saudi Arabia too. Erma, the mom of the house, taught me how to make Arabic flatbread and stuffed grape leaves. I love her."

His eyes get big. "So you know a little about my culture?" He smiles.

"Well, a little, I guess."

Pepper disappears with Dominic while Adnan leads me to an outdoor dining area. The wooden decks are massive. The sun reflects off the crystal and silver on the table. There are more wineglasses than I have ever seen in one place. The flower arrangements are gorgeous. White roses are mixed with eucalyptus and pine.

"Welcome to the *Nabila*, Gilles. I'm so glad you came."

"What does *Nabila* mean?" I ask.

"The boat is named after my daughter, Nabila, who just turned eighteen." Who would ever guess that later this ship would belong to the Sultan of Brunei and then Donald Trump? "Last night's party was for her."

"Oh, is she here?"

"No, she's on shore tonight."

Dominic and Pepper reappear and Adnan offers, "Girls, let me take you down to dress for dinner. Come, follow me." He leads us downstairs to a room lined with closets filled with couture gowns, and then he leaves. I am stunned, but Pepper takes it in stride. "What are you gonna wear?" she asks casually.

"Are you serious? What am I going to wear?" I shake my head and try to get a grip. "Do we just pick something? For real?"

"Yes." She laughs. "Pick out whatever you want." She's already browsing.

I can't believe my eyes—Dior, Yves Saint Laurent, Lanvin, Ungaro, Valentino, Chloé, Nina Ricci, and Chanel. All of the hand-sewn couture collections are here. They are all runway size and have only been worn once on a Paris catwalk. I choose a knee-length, delicate, silky, gray Lanvin dress with a tight bodice and spaghetti straps. I pick out some strappy metallic silver shoes that are a perfect fit. Pepper wears a tight, red strapless dress—of course.

We bounce back upstairs to join Adnan; Dominic and his wife, Ines; and two of Adnan's sons at the big round dining table out on the deck. Adnan pulls out the chair next to him for me. His young sons sit to his right. They're beautiful, with dark hair and eyes and olive skin.

A waiter in a white ship's crew uniform pours still water and bubbly water, while another pours champagne. We are served crab and lobster. White wine is poured. When we finish the seafood, we are given an entremets of frozen fruit topped with a mint leaf in a tiny crystal glass with a tiny silver spoon. My confusion is obvious, and Adnan informs me, "Oh, Gilles, this is a palate cleanser to prepare your mouth for our next course. Go ahead, eat it."

I am baffled by the multiple sets of silverware. I have no clue which ones to use. Now I have still water, bubbly mineral water, champagne, and white wine. I eat the seafood and the mini "dessert." Now it is time for the main course of lamb and vegetables, which evidently means I need red wine. I have five glasses full and counting. After the lamb, there is a salad and a dessert of fresh berries with ice cream and liqueur in crystal goblets. Then we are served port, cognac, and espresso. I try to act natural.

Adnan speaks energetically and proudly about his boys, his older kids, and his new boat, which has recently been christened. I imagine one of those huge champagne bottles smashing on the ship's hull and a big party after. I just met these people, but I already feel like I have missed out on something, as if I should have been there too.

I never met such an elegant man. Adnan is intelligent, worldly, and laughs easily. He has a kind of peaceful strength. I wish I had that. As we finish our espresso, the boys' nanny comes to collect them. Adnan leans in. "Gilles, can I show you around the boat?"

"Yes, of course!" I want to see all of it. He takes my hand and leads me on a private tour. With heels on, I am seven or eight inches taller than him. My being so much taller would intimidate most men, but not Adnan. He's obviously not easily rattled. The sun is setting as we walk the expanse of the ship and decks. He takes me to the engine room, set low in the ship's hull with massive shining machines, pipes, and gauges. He takes me to the ship's hospital, stating proudly that this is the only ship in the world where heart surgery can be performed. It's clear to me he was involved in the design and building of the ship because he seems to know every detail.

He shows me the navigation and control room, filled with high-tech instruments and maps. He gets excited over the mechanical and technological things. I feel so comfortable around him, and the energy that flows between us is electrifying.

He brings me to his daughter Nabila's room, which is decorated in red-and-white stripes like a peppermint candy circus tent. I think it is gaudy and dizzying. We take another elevator up to his master bedroom, where an illuminated glass triangle sculpture is mounted on a pedestal in the entryway. (I didn't know his business was called Triad Holding Company, thus the triangle.) His bedroom is massive, and his bed looks larger than a king-size. The bedspread is made of chinchilla fur, which is hard to imagine, and softer than air. He tells me his bathroom sink is solid gold, and the doorknobs are gold-plated.

There are hidden revolving walls and secret passageways, like in a James Bond movie (*Never Say Never Again* was filmed here). The living and entertaining rooms are dotted with gold-trimmed black lacquer tables between modern taupe leather couches. With the push of a button, he shows me how the formal dining room transforms into a conference room. There is even a movie theater with a big screen.

We return to the deck, where night has fallen. The sky sparkles with stars, the hills of Cannes twinkle, and the sea shimmers in the moonlight.

He points. "The helicopter is up there, and we have three speed-boats for waterskiing."

"Waterskiing? I love to ski! Could we ski together sometime? It's one of my favorite things in the world." Is this really happening? Boating at the Colorado River in Arizona were some of the best times of my childhood.

"Yes, of course," he says.

Walking along the chrome railing on the side deck, we notice boats below with flashing cameras and people waving and yelling, "*Bonne nuit!*" So, we wave too.

"They come every night to look at the boat. It's a beautiful night." He turns his attention away from the water below. "Tell me about you, Jill. What is your passion? What are your favorite things to do? Who are you, Jill? I want to know everything about you, you beautiful girl. Shall we go inside? Come, I'll show you my disco."

I am stunned that he is actually interested in who I am—and not just on the outside. It is truly shocking. I am becoming smitten so fast. I love his warm, sweet face, and his big eyes. I don't want this evening to end, ever. The age difference isn't registering. I feel electric.

Holding my hand, we walk around to the other side of the boat and into the disco, closing the door behind us. A DJ is playing music and colored lights reflect off a disco ball. A metal side door opens suddenly and a boatload of girls come dancing in. I spot a model I know from California, with whom I'd filmed *The Misadventures of Sheriff Lobo*—a seventies sitcom. As we say hello, I quickly note that these are not top-tier models. They are more the kind that hang around the Playboy Mansion. I want to be alone with Adnan. Thankfully, he rescues me.

"Gilles, can I call you Jill, or do you prefer Gilles?"

"Either way is good. Everybody calls me Gilles in France, but it's a man's name. Back home, I'm Jill. So, whatever you want."

"Okay, Jill, let's go someplace quiet so we can talk. It's too loud in here."

It is becoming obvious that Adnan is powerful. I mean, who has a ship like this? Part of me wants to downplay it and part of me is intoxicated by it. It is flattering to be the object of his intense interest and attention, and even more important—he makes me laugh. It's hard to describe the overwhelming serenity that envelops us. I'm wide-awake and totally at peace. How can he have this effect on me?

He guides me to a tiny, dimly lit room with a low ceiling that feels cozy and cave-like. We sit close on a small sofa facing each other, and before I can say anything he confesses, "I have to be honest with you. I know it's not fair, but I know everything about you." He closes his eyes, waiting for my response.

I am taken aback. "No, you don't. How could you know anything about me?" I am sure.

"Trust me, I do. You don't believe me?"

"No, I don't. No one even knows where I am most of the time."

"Okay . . . you were born in Lynwood, California. Your dad is a fireman who grew up in Hollywood. You had very good grades in school. You arrived in Paris this past February. You worked in the swimwear industry in Los Angeles. . . . Do I need to go on?"

As my eyes grow wider, he explains, "I had to have you checked out before you came on the boat. My security team insists on it."

I throw him a puzzled look. "You're kidding, right?" This is the strangest thing I've ever heard. By the looks of the ship, it is clear he could pull some strings, but what does it matter? I have nothing to hide. It is weird though, and knocks me off balance for a few minutes.

He abruptly changes the subject. "So, what are your goals in life?"

"I'm just modeling for right now." I am still confused by all the talk about security. Why does he need security?

"You're only twenty. You have time, don't you?"

"I guess. So you obviously know about me, but what about you? How old are you? Are you divorced? How many kids do you have?"

"I turned forty-four in July, and yes, I'm in the middle of a divorce, but we have a good relationship. I was angry at first, but it's going better now. We threw a huge divorce party on the boat for the kids. We didn't want them to be sad about us splitting up, so instead, we celebrated. Even though we're not together, we're both still their parents."

"Wow, that puts a fresh spin on it. What a great idea. I bet the kids liked it. How many kids do you have again?"

"I have five. Nabila is the oldest, my only daughter, and I have four sons, Mohammed and Khalid, and the youngest ones, Hussein and Omar, were at dinner tonight."

"They're so cute and well mannered. Very impressive."

"Now it's my turn," he adds lightly. "Have you ever kissed a girl?"

"What?"

"Have you ever kissed a girl?" he says, laughing.

He'd been forthcoming, so I say, "Yes, but only once in junior high."

He smiles big. "Tell me more. How far did you two go?"

"We were in junior high school and drunk. I kissed her on the lips—just a peck. I felt guilty after, like I had done something terrible. I apologized, but she didn't even remember it."

"Are you sure that was all you did?"

"Yes, I'm sure." I change the subject. "So, if you're from Saudi

Arabia, how did you learn to speak English? And were you born in Saudi Arabia?"

"Yes, I was born in Mecca, Saudi Arabia. I went to school in Egypt, then left school early to go to college at Chico State and Stanford in California. Because my father was the personal physician to King Abdul Aziz Al Saud of Saudi Arabia, I had a lot of connections, and I started exporting Chevy trucks to Saudi Arabia, and then Caterpillar tractors for construction projects. I made my first million dollars by seventeen. Then I exported aircraft with my friend Howard Hughes."

"Wow, I never thought about how countries got their trucks and tractors."

We talk through the night, covering everything—nothing is off-limits. I tell him about my jealous ex-boyfriend, Jack. He tells me that the party at Le Pirate had cost $25,000 and that it cost something like $400,000 each month to keep the boat going.

I explain how I used to sneak over to my Saudi Arabian neighbors' house all the time and how it was so peaceful there that I couldn't stay away. I tell him how Erma, the mom, used coffee grounds on her kids' wounds instead of bandages, as a temporary scab, and how she let me go with her to the park to pick olives and grape leaves. I'd go over just to fold laundry with her. She was so sweet, and I wished that my mom were like her.

I am telling Adnan things I have never told anybody. I haven't felt a connection this strong with anyone, male or female, in years. He doesn't try to kiss me in that little room, which makes me trust him even more. I am getting sleepy and want to curl up in his lap and continue the conversation with my eyes shut. But I don't. I lean on a pillow.

"Do you know what time it is?" I ask.

He pulls up his shirtsleeve to look at his watch and laughs in disbelief. "It's five in the morning!" We can't believe it.

"It seems like we've only been in here for an hour. No wonder my eyes are having a hard time staying open. I better go to bed. I don't mean to assume anything, but can Pepper and I sleep here? And do you know where she is?"

"I'm sure she's already in bed. I'll call Keith and find out what room she's in." He picks up the phone on the table. "*Oh, oui, la chambre verte, merci.*"

"Come, I'll show you to your room. You girls are in the green room." He gives me a big hug on the couch and gets up, reaching his hands out to help me up. He opens the steel door, and we duck our heads under the curved metal doorway. He walks me to my room and kisses my cheeks. "Good night, Gilles. I hope to see you soon." He doesn't try to kiss my mouth, but I really want him to.

Pepper emerges from the shower, hair wrapped in a towel, and jumps in bed with me. "Can you believe this boat?" she says. "Where were you? With Adnan?"

I nod. "We had so much fun. It's strange. I feel like I've known him forever." Pepper tries to turn off the lights, but when she clicks the remote, a television pops up from a cabinet at the foot of the bed. She pushes another button and shades cover the windows. Finally, she hits the one for the lights.

My body is tired, but my heart is pumping and my mind is buzzing. I try to wrap my head around what is happening, and eventually fall asleep. An hour later there is a knock at the door.

"*Mademoiselles*, time to wake up—you need to leave for your flight!" We force ourselves out of bed, climb down the stairs on the side of the huge ship, and into a speedboat. It is totally silent outside. The water is still as glass and the sun is just peeking out. As we speed away, it feels like a tether is holding me to Adnan, sleeping in his bed.

Pepper quizzes me in the car and on the plane back to Paris. "Are you sure you didn't sleep with him? You're not telling me everything."

"Really," I say, raising my eyebrows. "We just talked. Just because you sleep with everybody you meet doesn't mean I do."

Ruby and me in Halkidiki, Greece, summer 1980

QUEEN JEWELRY

September 1980, Paris and Greece

Paris is cold and rainy, and I force myself back into work mode. Memories of the pirate party, our intense conversations, dinner on the boat, his beautiful skin and eyes . . . Adnan is distracting me from my work! I have a fifth interview for a magazine shoot in Greece. Really? They need to see me five times for one job?

Adnan calls a few days later, inviting me to lunch at his home in Paris. He lives at 8 Avenue Montaigne, not far from Dior. A guard takes me upstairs to Adnan and Dominic. I wonder why Dominic is here. Adnan rushes over and gives me a big warm hug. Dominic kisses my cheeks, then Adnan gives me a tour of the house—mansion actually. He takes me through the exquisitely decorated bedrooms, bathrooms, and sitting rooms. I'll never forget the massive bathroom with the Turkish tub covered in green-and-gold mosaic, with the solid gold faucet. We pass through room after room, but his favorite things are always tech gadgets. Somehow, he has access to products that I've never even seen on the market. He demonstrates how his laser-disc player plays movies and music videos.

We join Dominic in the dining room, where his chef has prepared an informal lunch. Adnan sits at the end of a long dining table with me on one side and Dominic on the other. During lunch Adnan peruses divorce documents. He talks about Soraya, his ex-wife, wanting a community property settlement through California law. I don't understand these legal terms, and am surprised he's sharing this private document with me. The fact that he's so open makes me feel closer to him.

He then pulls out several jewelry catalogs from Van Cleef & Arpels, Boucheron, and Cartier, filled with jewels a queen would wear. A necklace that looks like a ribbon is set with hundreds of emeralds and surrounded by diamonds. There are chandelier earrings dripping with sparkling diamonds that look like drops of water. He turns the pages and he asks me, "What do you think of this? Do you like this one? Emeralds or sapphires? Rubies or diamonds?" I never would have assumed he could be shopping for me. He hands me the booklets. "Tell me which ones you like." I sit in my ripped T-shirt, jeans, and white moccasins, flipping through the "queen jewelry."

"I don't know. They're all pretty. But I do like this one more than that one." Was he seriously gonna buy this stuff?

He continues to read over his divorce documents. I'm sure the whole thing has got to be painful. I'm sorry for his pain, but glad he's divorced, because how could I be with him otherwise? I love spending time with him above just about anything. After lunch, I'm driven home in a Rolls-Royce limo.

✦

Three models, including me, two stylists, an editor, and a photographer all head to Halkidiki, Greece, on the Aegean Sea. Ruby, my red-haired ex-roommate, is one of the models.

On the first night, Ruby passes out cold with her head landing sideways in her bowl of soup and we have to carry her to her room. By the next morning, everyone in the hotel is sick, including the hotel staff. The photographer, Pierre, and I are the only ones who haven't contracted this horrible bug. I decide to wait it out at the beach, waterskiing, windsurfing, and swimming in the crystal clear water. Thankfully the boat driver is okay.

Five days in, everyone's still sick, so Pierre decides that we'd better start shooting. Since it's only the two of us, he begins an intense flirting campaign with me. We've got a strong connection and I'm flattered by the attention, but knowing he's married, I don't act on the chemistry. Instead, I walk the narrow line between refusing his puppy-dog advances and not pissing him off. When he threatens to climb over the balcony into my room, I don't know if he's serious or teasing. He turned out to be harmless and a lot of fun to work with.

As everyone gradually improves, we pull together to finish the job. Heading to the countryside, we stop for flocks of sheep and shepherds crossing the road. A village behind the hills had been established close to the sea for fishing and trade yet hidden from pirates. Brightly painted homes look like they have survived earthquakes and bombings. With their entire facades ripped off and open to the sea air, we can see the modest furnishings inside many of them. In the village square, leather-skinned men smoke and drink espresso, play cards and dice. When I need a toilet break at a café, it turns out to be a plastic bucket in a wood shack. Their poverty humbles me, yet their spirits are generous and warm. A pack of kids follow us around, showing us photos of "Charlie's Angels," thinking we three models look like them.

We return to the sea to a bay filled with colorful, hand-painted fishing boats. Fishermen are pulling in their nets full of fish. While I'm changing my clothes in the open air, Pierre suggests we do a topless shot. In France, many summer fashion magazine covers are topless and I've always thought they were beautiful and tasteful. I'm nervous but I do it anyway.

A couple of weeks later, we all meet at the studio to view the photos from Greece. They're all beautiful! Pierre is so talented. As I look through the slides, I come upon the topless ones. I try to see them objectively but can't. I flash to my dad's *Playboy* magazines and can't stop drawing a parallel between the two.

I'm totally unable to look at them for what they are—beautiful, artistic photos of a young woman in Greece. Everyone thinks they're pretty, but I can't handle it. I panic and slice the slides up with scissors into the trash bin.

Shaken, I walk away from the light box and mill around the studio. Pierre's wife tells me privately, "Many years ago, when my husband and I began this business, he never looked at the models in that way, you know what I mean? They were only a tool to him, like a prop, a table or a chair. But now he looks at them differently and he treats me like a chair."

Boulevard Magenta just before my zipper broke,
Paris, 1980

MY BROKEN ZIPPER

I haven't heard from Adnan in a couple of weeks and am wondering if he has forgotten about me. I don't understand these spaces in between. At last, Pepper calls saying Adnan has invited her and me to dinner at his Paris home.

I can't wait to see him. I wear a strapless red velvet jumpsuit I bought at the Clignancourt flea market with matching red satin shoes. I braid the front of my hair and crisscross it on top, Frida Kahlo–style, leaving the back long.

Pepper and I are escorted to his reception hall, where four girls younger than me are waiting too. *Why are they here?* Pepper takes it in stride. Adnan joins us and we all have a drink around a small round cocktail table. After saying our friendly hellos, Adnan gets the conversation going by asking, "So, which of you girls has had a lesbian experience?"

One girl, who looks like she is in high school, is so embarrassed that she throws her jacket over her head. Then he says, "Oh, you must have if you're so embarrassed—that means you have!" I was hoping he wouldn't pull me into this again.

Right then, I feel my zipper slide down. Cool air hits my skin, and soon my entire backside is exposed. Cheap flea market clothes!

I'm mortified. I whisper to Pepper, "Come to the bathroom, some-thing's happening with my zipper!"

She looks at my back. "Oh, shit! Your zipper broke!" She breaks out laughing.

"Will you help me hold it together please, and come with me?" I am trying to act sophisticated. Pepper follows, laughing, holding my outfit together.

She tries pulling the zipper up, but it's broken. "This zipper is definitely not going back up."

Adnan is listening at the door. "Girls, do you need my help?"

"Her clothes are broken!" Pepper says, giggling.

"What am I gonna do, Pepper?"

Adnan says playfully, "What's going on in there? Open the door, girls." I open it slightly and peek out. He's standing there with a huge grin. He lives for this stuff. "Come with me." He takes my hand and leads me to a closet that's as big as a bedroom. Each wall is an alcove and filled with beautiful gowns. "Let's see, I bet we can find you something to wear in here." I can't believe the glamorous dresses before me. I see some of the tags—Paris Haute Couture. The inner fashion designer in me is freaking out. He starts pulling them out. "Do you see anything you like?"

"This is so embarrassing." I stand holding the front of my jump-suit with the back gaping open. I want to dive in and try on bunches of these dresses, but how am I supposed to act in this situation? I wait for him.

"How about this? It has tulips. Oh, here's a red skirt that goes with it. Try it on."

I take them to the bathroom and hang them up on a hook. I'm so excited! The blouse is completely covered in hand-beaded red tulips with green leaves and must weigh three pounds. The label sewn into the neck reads Emanuel Ungaro Couture Paris. Unbe-lievable. The skirt is made of red silk and light as a feather. Its label reads Christian Dior Couture Paris. It hangs from my waist like an upside-down tulip. I can't believe I'm wearing Dior and Ungaro. They fit like they're made for me. I open the door.

Adnan is waiting. "Darling, you look beautiful. I like this much better on you."

"It's really beautiful. Are you sure I can wear it?"

"Yes, of course. Come on, let's join the party."

Classical music fills the dining room. The long table is set with a feast fit for a king—candles, crystal, and silver platters of seafood, vegetables, and fruit. Two chefs enter carrying a roast lamb on a massive platter. They set the lamb in the middle of the table and carve it. It's like the Roman Empire.

Adnan busily entertains everyone in the room. All of us girls waltz around together. Finally, Adnan and I dance alone, and somehow we wind up chasing each other around the room, under the bar, and behind the tables. He does not act forty-four and is more fun than any guy I've ever met. At the door, at the end of the night, he kisses my cheeks and hands me an exotic-looking, prickly piece of fruit. "Do you know what this is?"

"No, I don't."

"It's a special fruit. Next time I see you, I want you to tell me what it is."

He escorts me, tucking me into the back of a black Rolls-Royce limousine, instructing the driver of my address at 76 Boulevard Magenta. I can't believe I'm being driven through Paris in this fancy car in this fancy dress. I never want tonight to end and I can't wait to see Adnan again. I put my skeleton key into the big wood door and make my way through the cobblestoned courtyard, and up the dark stairway. I unlock the apartment, tiptoe down the hall, and get in bed. I take off my clothes and study the beading on the blouse, trying to figure out how many months it would take to sew all these tiny beads on by hand.

I lie back on my pillow, studying the mysterious, spiky, orange fruit. Why did he give this to me? What does it mean? Is it poison? I finally give up and pull my blankets around my neck in my tiny bed in my dirty room, feeling like a princess for the first time in my life.

Sparkly dress in Paris, 1980

BUTTER CROISSANTS

I have no idea I am in for a radical change. Like everyone else, I'm preoccupied with the endless details and tasks that fill my days. I'm finally enjoying modeling, but after realizing that success won't instantly solve all of my problems or give me that magic feeling I'm looking for, I'm not willing to die for it. Or sacrifice my dignity and peace.

Every time I see myself in another magazine or on a poster, it is confirmed. The less I care, the more everybody wants to hire me. Go figure!

I keep up my daily practice of sitting for hours in cafés writing. As I walk alone through the streets, listening to my inner voice, I lend a hand and a smile to any- and everyone who needs one. Paris is starting to love me right back, and I am truly happy. I feel more and more that this is my home.

Oftentimes, I stop to pray and meditate in the beautiful and peaceful cathedrals. I light a candle and watch mine burn along with all the others that people have come to light. Even though I don't know how I'm supposed to pray, I pray. I don't rush through these meditative, peaceful things. I do them slowly, taking my sweet time. I can sit in a church for over an hour without being bored. These essential elements add up to peace and happiness for me.

I feel more rooted inside myself than ever before. I'm no longer a directionless, dead, dry leaf blowing in the wind through the streets of Paris.

Now that I am in high demand as a model, I have the confidence to make changes that are way overdue. I'm done with the games at Paris Planning and decide to switch agencies.

I hear that Karin Models is good, and Jean Luc Brunel, head of the agency, signs me immediately. Pepper and Gerald are shocked. They warn that Jean Luc doesn't have as much power as them. But they are dead wrong. Karin books me instantly for good French and Italian editorial. I should have switched sooner.

Work is going well, and I have made gains in my "personal peace project." But as a young woman, I'm lonely. Scarlett is gone, and most of my time is spent traveling alone.

My sexual desires have been nagging at me, but I won't have sex with just anyone. I have to be in a loving relationship. I want to date Adnan, but he hasn't called me since giving me the thorny, yellow fruit. Does he even think about me? There are lots of male models around, but they seem like another species, too pretty and skinny. I have never felt comfortable with overly handsome men. Maybe I don't think I deserve a man like that, or maybe I'm plain old intimidated.

◆

Ruby invites me over to her boyfriend Will's house for dinner. He's an English photographer who changes my opinion that all photographers are grungy and grubby. He's handsome, in his late thirties, funny, sweet, and can hire Ruby for jobs directly without even a go-see. Some of his friends from London come to the dinner too—sadly, none of whom I am attracted to.

After dessert, we play charades and his friend Benjamin pulls out a joint, lights it, and hands it to me. "Oh, no, thanks, I haven't done that since high school." They all take a hit and pass it to me again.

"Okay, maybe a little." We laugh uncontrollably until I fall asleep on Will's couch.

In the morning, Will sweeps through the front door with a bag of warm croissants. *Lucky Ruby—a boyfriend and breakfast.* "Mornin', love. Fancy a croissant? I swear they're the best in Paris."

The brown bag is butter-stained, and I can smell the croissants from the couch. "I try not to eat them, but I really want to." He hands me one. I break it open and take a long sniff. "These are dangerous. Good thing I don't live around here."

"We have 'em every morning. Can't start my day without 'em. Espresso?"

"No, thanks, gotta get ready for work. Thanks for dinner last night, and thanks for this."

I leave Will's pretty apartment and walk the narrow streets with the granite curbs, eating my personal piece of paradise.

The market owners are stacking crates of fresh vegetables, and baristas are starting their day by hosing off the sidewalks in front of their cafés. All I can think about is love. I want to be in love like Ruby and Will.

I approach my favorite, most beautiful bridge in Paris, the Pont Alexandre III. I stop halfway across and watch the rising sun reflect shimmery orange onto the Seine as I lean on the cold, damp stone. When I first came to Paris, love was the last thing on my mind. I never planned to stay this long, but now I feel differently.

Paris is my true home, and I may never live anywhere else but here. If I had a boyfriend we'd be here on this beautiful bridge together, watching the sunrise and the birds diving for fish. He would hold me and kiss me tenderly, and the beauty of Paris wouldn't be wasted.

✦

"Gilles! *Le téléphone est pour vous!*" Madame yells in her monotone Vietnamese French.

"*Oui, allô.*" Madame's television is blaring in the background.

"Wow, Jill, look at you talking all French."

"Jack? Is that you?" I am shocked to hear his voice.

"Yeah, it's me. I'm coming to Paris to see you."

My heart sinks. "What?"

"I'm coming to bring you home. Let's take this to the next level. I really miss you. I'm making a lot of money now. I can take care of you. I bought two machine shops."

"I don't want you to take care of me. How did you buy two shops?"

"I've been dealing and saving all the money."

I never would have dreamed he would sell drugs. "You're crazy. You're gonna get killed or go to prison!"

"It's okay. I sleep with a gun under my pillow, and when the shops are up and running, I'll stop." He sounds paranoid. This does not sound like the Jack I know.

"No, don't come."

"I already bought a plane ticket. I'll be there in two weeks. You can't stop me. I'm going to find you!" He laughs, but it isn't funny.

I panic and try to act strong, but my heart is in my throat. "You don't speak French, you don't know where I live, you'll never find me here. Paris is a big city. We broke up. I live here now." He never takes no for an answer, and I am scared. "I gotta go. Don't come. I don't want you to come. 'Bye."

I hang up the phone, with my heart beating in my ears. I don't need this shit right now. I go back to my room and write in my Bible, asking for help. I have no idea where my life is going, but I know I'm done with him.

I am still writing when the phone rings again.

"Gilles, *le téléphone est pour vous encore!*" Madame giggles.

I run to her room. "*Oui, allô?*"

"Hey, it's Dominic. We're here in Paris and you'll never guess who's with us. Margaux Hemingway! But that's not why I called. Adnan wants me to invite you to Spain and the Canary Islands with us."

My head is spinning from Jack, but I know I miss Adnan. "I'd love to come, but how much will it cost?"

"Don't worry about it. Adnan will cover it."

"Are you sure? I can pay my way."

"Jill, I'm sure. He can afford it."

Adnan and me in Marbella, Spain, 1980

THE CONTRACT

September and October 1980, Paris and Spain

Dominic's wife, Ines, a Swedish former model, greets me at the door of their fancy 7th arrondissement apartment. It's the picture of luxury, with polished marble floors and modern furniture. Dominic comes to say hello and then goes to finish packing.

The stairwell is plastered with glamorous party photos on boats and beaches, all the things I miss the most about California—except fancier. A guest room has photos and a modeling composite pinned to the wall. She's my friend and fellow Wilhelmina model from Los Angeles. "That's Gwen's room. She stays here when she's in Paris," Ines says.

"I know Gwen. We worked together a lot in LA." I'm confused why she has a room here.

Ines's niece, Nora, joins us, and the four of us take a limo to the airport and board Adnan's private DC-9. We just stroll right onto the plane—no ticket, no parking lot, no lines. We relax into tan leather reclining chairs, while we are served drinks and snacks.

We land in Málaga, Spain, and are driven through the coastal towns of Marbella and Puerto Banús. Images of my last trip flash through my head—the bomb threat, the Spanish army, the tanks, and the insane and probably fake photographer. Maybe this trip could cover up those memories.

We wind up into the hills of Andalusia to Benahavis, where Adnan's home is set on five thousand acres of wildlife preserve. It is called La Baraka, "blessings of God." The Spanish-style home has a curved driveway with a fountain and beautiful garden. On the porch stands a life-size giant taxidermy polar bear and lion. Elephant tusks form an arch in the entryway, and antelope and deer antlers adorn the walls. Adnan bought the property from Omar Sharif, Dominic explains, as he shows me to my room.

"Adnan wants you to sleep in here, and Nora will sleep in the yellow room." The floor is rough-hewn slate, cold for a bedroom. The twin beds are topped with stiff zebra skins, and an actual zebra leg lamp sits on the desk by the sliding glass door. Underneath is a real elephant foot that has been hollowed out to use for a trash can. A lion-skin rug is on the floor, his face frozen in his last roar. This room is cold and creepy. I think it is disgusting, and I hope it was Omar Sharif's taste and not Adnan's.

Nora's room, on the other hand, is decorated in yellow Laura Ashley floral. I hang out there instead. As night falls, the nocturnal animals outside come to life. Birds squawk, and I hear what sounds like bears growling and monkeys screeching. The estate manager slides heavy wood shutters over all the doors and windows to keep us safe. Nora and I look at each other in disbelief. Finally, she says in English, with her heavy Swedish accent, "I am not sleeping in here alone with wild animals right outside."

I crack up, nodding in agreement. "I'll stay with you—have you seen my room? It's terrifying!" We turn out the lights and giggle nervously at the noises outside, but soon I fall into a deep sleep. I have learned to sleep anywhere, anytime.

In the morning, the scent of coffee and freshly baked bread coaxes us into the dining room, where the chef has a full breakfast waiting. The view outside the sliding glass doors is incredible. Just outside, from the pool, you can see the Mediterranean, the Strait of Gibraltar, the Rock of Gibraltar, and even Morocco. It is so beautiful that it doesn't look real.

Adnan flew his masseur, Tony, over to work on us, and even his chiropractor pays us a visit. I have a broken tailbone from a gymnastics fall in junior high and it always causes my lower back to ache. The chiropractor does an adjustment on me and it feels so much better. My back is straight and my posture good for the first time in years.

But then we go to the horse stables on the property and ride Adnan's Arabian horses. It doesn't occur to me that it could mess up my back, but something crunches and cracks and I feels like it's broken all over again. I am in terrible pain. I'm not a complainer though, and try to go on as usual. Tony's massages help.

We tour the town, shopping for souvenirs and eating lunch outside by the docks. The chef prepares delicious, healthy meals daily. Nora and I stargaze through the powerful telescope on the patio. I have never seen the moon or Venus in such detail. I don't have to worry about a thing. Everything is taken care of. As each day passes, I relax a little deeper.

◆

After nearly a week, in the middle of the night, I feel someone shaking me. Dominic whispers, "There she is. She's right here."

Adnan whispers playfully, "I've been looking all over for you." He takes my hand. "Shhh, come, come." He leads me to a different wing of the house. "You were supposed to be in the animal room. I even went to Dominic and Ines's bed and pulled off all the covers looking for you. I thought you were having a threesome." He's giggling and way too alert.

I'm so sleepy that his words don't register. He brings me to his bedroom and we sit on the bed while I try to wake up.

"I came to you as soon as I could. I just flew in."

"Oh you did? That's sweet," I say, groggily.

"I missed you so much. Did you miss me? What have you been doing since I saw you?"

"Just working a lot, until I came here, that is."

"You don't have another boyfriend, do you?" he teases.

"No, no. I don't."

"Good. I've been traveling so much since I saw you—so many meetings in so many countries. But enough about work, let me make you a bath."

He makes a beautiful bath with scented bubbles and vanilla candles. I take off my oversize T-shirt and panties and slide in. Adnan sits on a stool next to the tub. He is engaged and attentive, listening intensely and asking me deep, challenging questions. I'm still sleepy.

He asks, "When did you lose your virginity?"

"Oh my god, really?"

"Yes, really."

"Well, I've never told anyone this, but it was in the back of a truck at a drive-in movie, with my boyfriend, Jack."

"How old were you?"

"Eighteen."

"How many men have you been with?"

"Just Jack." I don't mention my unwanted sex with Gerald. I'm still confused about that whole thing.

"So, I hear you rode my Arabian horses. Did you enjoy them?"

"Yes, they're beautiful and so sweet." I don't mention my back is aching.

"And have you met the Count? He's a character, a good friend of mine."

"Umm, no, not yet. Is he coming over?"

"Yes, I'm not sure when. Do you like the bubble bath? The scent?"

"Yes, what is it?"

"It's mint. I buy it directly from Morocco. It's my favorite." Then he asks, "Do you want some cocaine?"

"No. I don't." I sink down to my chin in the bubbles.

"Come on, it'll be fun. Have some." He pours a pile on the side of the tub and maneuvers it into two fat lines with a razor blade. Then he rolls an American one-hundred-dollar bill. "Just try a little, it's not dangerous." He snorts a line. I am afraid of cocaine and have always refused it. "Just take a little, it'll wake you up."

I don't know why, but eventually I take the rolled bill and snort about a third of a line. My nose feels cold and burns at the same time, then my heart starts racing, and my mind becomes super clear. I feel happy and awake, like him. We talk even more and he says, "I don't do this very often. Just to have fun sometimes."

"That's good," I say.

I dry off and he hands me a long dark blue Arab caftan, a *thaub*, matching the one he is wearing. We sit on his bed, talking and laughing.

Every single emotion I feel for him is present in that bed. I have been gradually falling in love with him and haven't stopped thinking about him since the pirate party, the night on his ship, the times in Paris, and the thorny fruit. I keep wishing he'd make a move on me, but the fact that he hasn't only makes me want him more. My sex drive has been raging, and my emotions longing for love. Everything bubbles to the surface, and for the first time since I moved to Paris, I am sure I want to make love.

"The only difference between you and me is that I'm a Muslim and you're a Christian."

I look at him confused. "I'm not a Christian."

"You're American, so you're Christian."

"I wasn't raised with religion," I say. "My parents hate religion." I feel so ashamed of my ignorance.

"Do you have any brothers and sisters?" I ask, changing the subject.

"I have two brothers and a sister who live in the US, and a sister in London." I later learn that his sister, Samira Khashoggi, is married to the Harrods businessman and owner of the Paris Ritz Hotel, Mohammed Al Fayed, and they are the parents of Dodi Al Fayed, who died tragically with Princess Diana in Paris.

"So, why did you get divorced?"

"My wife had an affair. Several actually. So I found ten girls to have sex with at the same time, as revenge."

My eyes get big. "That's crazy, did you do it?"

"Yep, all eleven of us in one bed. I kicked a couple of them out at some point." He laughs. It is obvious to me that he is still hurt over his wife, Soraya. She bruised him badly. "I learned a valuable lesson though. I'll never marry in the traditional way ever again. I have another arrangement. It's not new. Thousands of years ago, so many men were killed in battle that there weren't enough men to care for all the women and children. I'm sure you've read about this in the Bible."

"No, but it sounds familiar." Maybe I heard it in history class?

"If a man was killed, his brother would take his brother's wife as his own and raise his brother's children. Women and children needed protection, food, and shelter. It was a necessity for men to take many wives. Today, in Saudi Arabia, among royalty and men of high esteem, it still goes on this way. These men are allowed to have three legal wives and eleven pleasure wives. Jill, I am one of these men." We're sitting crisscross applesauce in our *thaubs* on the bed.

I look him dead in the eyes, trying to remember all the details. His arrangement doesn't sound so strange, unusual maybe, but not strange. It seems like he is trying to justify or sell me on the idea of being with him, which isn't even necessary. I've already fallen for him and don't need any of his reasons. I push his speech to the back of my mind and focus on the intelligent, brown-eyed man with the long eyelashes in front of me.

"I want you to be my pleasure wife. I'd like to make a contract with you," he says very seriously.

"I don't need a contract." I shake my head.

"Please listen," he says, gently holding my face in his hands. "I will provide for all of your financial needs. You can travel with me anywhere. If you need me, call me. I will always call you back within twenty-four hours and send a plane to pick you up. If you stay with me for ten years, and you want to have my child, I will marry you in a legal ceremony and we'll have children together."

"You don't need to make promises. I just want to be with you."

He continues, "You can date other men as long as they're not from Saudi Arabia. It would be very embarrassing if I were at a dinner party with men from my country and we found out we were with the same woman." He acts hesitantly, unsure if I will accept his offer. "There is another advantage to being with me. I can introduce you to a young duke, lord, or prince. Don't fall in love with me. I'm too old for you. You need to marry a young prince, Jill. I'll find you a prince or duke to marry."

I am not even sure what a duke or lord is. *Can't we get on with this?* "I don't care about a contract or a duke or lord."

"But I do. Before I can kiss you, I need to make a contract with you. I want you to be my pleasure wife. Will you?"

"Yes." We start kissing and making out on the bed. I want to make love with him.

I stop and sit up. "Wait, I don't have any birth control."

"It's okay, I've had a vasectomy."

"Then how can you have more children?"

"The doctors took my sperm and froze it. It's kept in a sperm bank. I can get it whenever I want. So in ten years if you want to have a baby, we can." I had never heard of such a thing.

Finally, we make love. Our bodies flow together perfectly. We never sleep. I lie snuggled into his neck, my head on his shoulder, when he gets an idea. "Let's go hunting!"

"Hunting? Wow, where?"

"In the nature preserve—around the house."

"You're not going to kill anything, are you?"

"If I'm lucky I will."

"Oh, please don't."

"Come on, it'll be fun. Get dressed and meet me in the breakfast room."

I throw on jeans, a sweatshirt, and tennis shoes, and come out to a beautiful breakfast on the coffee table. How does the chef always know what's going on? Five bodyguards with submachine guns hanging across their chests stand around while I nibble and watch the sunrise. Adnan sits on the couch next to me and hands me a square, black leather envelope. I have never seen a leather envelope and have no idea what could be inside. I open it carefully to reveal a heart-shaped ring covered in diamonds and a necklace with diamond hearts all the way around. He puts the ring on my finger and fastens the necklace around my neck. I am glad it isn't the queen of England–style jewelry like the catalogs in his Paris home.

His driver pulls an open-topped Jeep around, we jump in and take off into the preserve surrounding the estate. When the men spot a beautiful antelope in the bushes a good distance away, they quietly roll to a stop. Adnan takes aim with his rifle, while I hold my breath, hoping he'll miss. Thankfully, he does. He also misses the long-horned sheep and the mountain goats.

After shooting, we go to the helipad for a tour of the area in his helicopter. The pilot drops us off at the harbor, where we jump in a superfast cigarette boat. We lie back on the engine cover holding hands, speeding and bobbing through the sea, laughing. Adnan has managed to push every single one of my happy buttons. Speedboats are my ultimate weakness. Then he takes me dress shopping.

He tells me he needs to attend meetings in another country, and that he would meet me in Kenya. The rest of us continue vacationing in Spain. Sabine, a quiet girl from Denmark, who is about my age with dark hair and blue eyes, joins us. I assume she is a friend of Dominic and Ines's. Adnan's friend, known as the Count, comes to visit. Jaime de Mora y Aragón is a dapper gentleman who looks a lot like Salvador Dalí. This man knows how to entertain a table. One day, while we all enjoy an al fresco lunch, he tells stories of fighting in a foreign war, and that instead of marijuana, they used to roll and smoke black tea and ground pepper. He rolls up one of his concoctions and we all try it. It seems to work a little.

I love spending time talking with Ines. She looks like a Swedish version of the seventies model Jerry Hall. She has an air of class and sophistication and seems so worldly and wise. She met Dominic while she was modeling in Paris. She says that she and her friends would scheme to meet a rich man by saving all their modeling money to splurge on a breakfast at the Hotel George V, where rich businessmen dined. That was how she met Dominic, as I remember. She also explains that Adnan had saved Dominic from some sort of financial trouble. Anyway, he works for Adnan now. Doing what, I don't know.

The whole dynamic with Dominic, Ines, and her niece makes me feel like I am in a family. I feel safe with them. Ines is like a glamorous mother, Dominic a handsome, manly father, and Nora a sister.

◆

I don't know if it's true because I wasn't there, but there are theories about Adnan's involvement in negotiating the release of the Iranian hostages after the November election. Ronald Reagan and George Bush worried that if they were released before the election, Jimmy Carter would be reelected. Some accounts say that Adnan was in Paris on my birthday, negotiating the October surprise. All I know for sure is that he left Spain on a business trip and was gone on my birthday, October 19.

I turn twenty-one in Marbella, about a week after becoming Adnan's pleasure wife. He's gone on business, and I'm still not sure what a pleasure wife is or whether to take the whole thing seriously.

I think about my friends in California, imagining what kind of crazy things we'd do together for my birthday. We'd probably head to Vegas and dance all night at a club. The chef prepares a special dinner and birthday cake. Everyone gives me little gifts, and we all go dancing at Jimmy'z disco. But tonight, I really miss my old friends, especially Scarlett.

Maasai welcoming Adnan to Kenya, 1980

LOVE IN AFRICA

October 1980, Kenya

We board Adnan's private DC-9 in Málaga, Spain, and head to
Nairobi, Kenya. We are each handed a *thaub* to wear. After a chef-
prepared meal, everyone but me climbs into beds that fold out from
the plane's walls. I'm too excited to sleep and instead sit between the
pilots in the cockpit, where we all talk for hours. I'm very curious
about the life of private jet pilots. Flying over Egypt, they point out
the Nile by the twinkling lights that snake along on either side. I
had always dreamed of seeing the Nile.

Just after sunrise, we stop to refuel in Cairo when, seemingly out
of nowhere, bayonet-wielding Egyptian soldiers, wearing military
uniforms and turbans, surround the plane. I am used to European
soldiers in modern uniforms that look more like suits, with machine
guns. These soldiers look like they're from another time period and
seem unpredictable.

Two military officers board and the general stands guard on the
plane, while the other takes our passports to the terminal. I watch
the soldiers out the window, and they watch us. Finally, he returns
with our passports and the general commands the soldiers to with-
draw. I am relieved when we take off again for Kenya.

In Nairobi, we transfer to a small prop plane for the short flight to Adnan's estate, where we land on an airstrip next to his house. Africa has always captivated me, yet I have only seen it on nature shows and in *National Geographic*. I always longed to see it in person. And an unexpected thing happens: The moment my feet hit the dirt, I feel rooted to this ground as if it were my home.

Iridescent blue-and-green peacocks roam the roof of Adnan's house, squawking and shaking their plumes. It is an American ranch–style home with white plaster and brown wood trim. The county of Laikipia is situated in the foothills of the Aberdares Mountains with a view of the snow-capped peaks of Mount Kenya. The property is called Ol Pejeta, an 110,000-acre private game conservancy—just one of four in Kenya.

Frank, the estate manager, introduces himself to Nora and me and offers to take us on a Jeep ride. Nora refuses, but I never say no to adventure. Frank and I jump in the open-air Jeep and take off into the brush on dirt trails. He stops at various crossroads to show me bones and tusks from warthogs. He tells me they mark cannibal territory and warns about evil spirits. He's obviously trying to scare me, but this kind of terrain is so similar to where I rode motorcycles in the deserts of California that it doesn't faze me at first.

Frank seems to take my calm nature as a challenge and drives faster and faster, crashing into and mowing over bushes and small trees. We plunge down ditches and hurl over rocks. The car's about to flip, and with no seat belt, my body slams into the windshield and side to side.

"Slow down! You're going to kill us! Please stop!" I scream.

He laughs like a demon. The more I plead, the faster he goes. When we finally make it back, I'm so pissed off at this idiot trying to prove his manhood. *Asshole*. When I tell Dominic he says, "Oh no, he's done that before. He took Adnan's kids on a wild ride once, and Adnan almost fired him. I'll let the chief know." I'm not satisfied with this answer, but move on.

"Well, when is he coming? I can't wait to see him." I try to calm down.

"He'll be here tomorrow." I can't wait.

Adnan's Kenya house is brand-new and construction has just finished. No one has even slept in it yet. We are to wait till Adnan arrives to stay in the house, so everyone is assigned to dilapidated construction trailers, the kind you drag behind a pickup truck to go camping. Luckily, I am used to camping. Nora and I share one.

Getting ready and dressing in Paris Couture for dinner in a grimy, old construction trailer is a weird world of opposites. Torches light our way through the surrounding property to the house, where wide porch steps lead to the grand living room with dark wood floors and white overstuffed furniture. A painting hanging over the fireplace of an oil pipe dripping black spots onto a pure white cheetah makes me wonder if Adnan is in the oil business. All I know is that he sells tractors, trucks, and airplanes to the Middle East.

The architect of this new home and his wife join us, along with Keith, Adnan's mild-mannered, sweet, gay butler.

As we gather for drinks in the living room, I become acutely aware of how quickly strangers can bond when they're isolated together in a foreign country. I've only been traveling with Dominic and Ines for a couple of weeks, yet I feel so connected to them. My guard isn't up. All I feel is pure trust and love for them.

Keith calls us to the dining room where the table is festively decorated with banana leaves, flowers, and candles. As we're served a creamy green soup, Keith says, "Guess what kind of soup this is—no hints." We shout, "Alligator? Fish? Turtle? Zucchini?" It's turtle. I'm becoming accustomed to eating all kinds of things. After all, eating frogs and snails is de rigueur in Paris.

After dinner, Nora and I tromp through the brush to our trailer. I unzip my glittery, black silk dress and climb between the sheets of the tiny cot. When I look up to turn out the light, I see a spider as large as a dinner plate. I leap out of bed and run back to the house to find an estate worker to get it out. When I close my eyes though, all I can think about are spiders.

The next day, we fly to Nairobi for supplies. We need pants, socks, and boots to protect us from bugs and snakes. Plus, we need to buy and start taking malaria pills. The dirt roads are a deep shade of terra-cotta, and clotheslines hang between shops and food stands. A rolling cart loaded with bananas thrills me; bunches hang along ropes strewn high. We visit the grand Jamia Mosque, with its silver-pointed domes gleaming in the sun.

Back at the house, the rumble of a plane sends us all out to the airstrip. Barefoot Kenyans in traditional Maasai attire—brightly printed batiks wrapped and tied, with layers of bright, hand-beaded necklaces and Halloween masks added to the mix—mob Adnan with singing, dancing, hugs, and kisses.

"Why are they so happy to see him? It's like the king has arrived," I ask Dominic.

"Adnan built a school for their kids. We're celebrating tonight."

Adnan's right-hand man, Bob Shaheen, and Tony, the masseur, arrive with him. I have never heard of an entourage, but I'm in one now. We are Adnan's portable family. Private planes, chefs, a masseur, and housemaids create a bubble of false security. Everything is taken care of, and all my energy is saved for him. I guess that was the plan, because Adnan and I go directly to his bedroom.

✦

The housemaids move our things from the trailers to the bedrooms in the house. Later that night, as we gather for drinks in the living room, I get a shocking glimpse of Adnan's power.

"Ronald Reagan is going to win the American presidential election," Adnan says confidently.

"How could you know that? The election hasn't even happened," I say.

Adnan, Bob, and Dominic laugh. "We know."

"What do you mean, you know?" I ask.

"You'll see," Bob says, laughing.

I don't understand their political conversations.

Ines tries to convince me that Adnan is, in fact, completely connected and intertwined with the American political power players.
Then she suggests, "Why don't you run for president, AK?" AK is
what close friends call him.

"I wouldn't want to be president. I can do so much more if I stay
behind the scenes." I wonder if a Saudi Arabian man could even run
for the American presidency.

The other topic of conversation tonight is Soraya, AK's ex-
wife. Everyone is speculating who she's seeing now. I keep hearing
Winston Churchill's name, among others. No one mentions that
she just gave birth to her daughter, Petrina Khashoggi, in July. Not
that I can remember anyway. Although guessing who the father is
is probably what started the whole conversation. (Soraya keeps the
identity of the birth father a mystery until Petrina figures out later,
through DNA testing, that Jonathan Aitken, the former English
politician, is her birth father.) It seems to me that Adnan is still hurt
over Soraya. Otherwise, why would he keep bringing her up or care
who she's dating?

✦

When we go on safari, I don't want to miss a thing so I stand up
through the roof of the Jeep. We pass a bridge with a handmade
sign that reads, ATTENTION! ALLIGATORS! A man has recently
been swallowed. My mind wanders to the two pools on the estate,
especially the black-bottomed one outside AK's bedroom. *Could an
alligator crawl in there?*

We venture into open terrain for miles and finally spot a herd of
giraffe munching the tops of acacia trees. They're so large and graceful they seem to move in slow motion. Herds of gazelle, bongo, and
zebra roam and play. There are huts made of mud and stone walls

with cone-shaped, palm-frond roofs. Two adorable young boys sit on theirs. We yell *"Jambo!"* to one another, then stop to throw them our extra clothes, as theirs are torn rags. The highlight of the safari is when we get to see a lion. He is majestic with his wild mane.

We visit the Safari Club that Adnan owns, and several animal preserves. We feed sugarcane to black rhino and watch water buffalo chill in the river. At Iris and Don Hunt's preserve, I get to bottle-feed an orphaned baby elephant and giraffe. Their house pets, two full-grown cheetahs, jump in and out of open windows and one sits with her front paws on my thighs while I sit on the couch! She licks my face with her sandpaper tongue. I'm beyond thrilled. In the plane back to the ranch, we spot a massive herd of elephant on the move. It's paradise on earth.

Most of my time is spent with Adnan in his bedroom. Elephant tusks adorn the entry table, and there's a breakfast nook that opens to a private pool. The bed linens are embroidered with African animals. Every detail is perfect. His closet has a complete wardrobe of formal suits, casual clothes, and *thaubs*. Again, his bathroom has solid gold faucets and sinks and bulletproof walls. Adnan explains, "Any wall where I stand for more than a few minutes must be armored." At least the bodyguards aren't here. "I'm tired of living in fear," he says. "I don't like traveling with bodyguards all the time."

The absolute wildness of Kenya is the perfect contrast to the softness of each other's skin. We crave each other. After making love yet again, Adnan brings me to his closet. We stand nude, as he opens his safe and pulls out a huge twenty-carat diamond ring. "I want you to have this." He slides it onto my ring finger.

My heart jumps, but not in a good way. It scares me somehow. I'm overwhelmed. "I can't. I'm sorry, it's too much!" I push it back into his hands. The jump from poor Paris model to twenty-carat diamonds is too big a spread.

"Why? I want you to have it. It means a lot to me."

"I'm sorry, really I can't." I think I offended him because his boy-ish excitement darkens as he returns it to the safe. Then he abruptly pulls a white dress shirt off a hanger.

"How about this? Can you take this?" I nod, looking at him as he wraps it around my shoulders. I feel like such a baby. I'm sure he's wondering what the hell is wrong with me.

"Did you ever figure out the kind of fruit I gave to you in Paris?"

"No, what was it?"

"An African horned melon, and here we are in Africa. Did you eat it?"

"No, I couldn't figure out how to open it or if it was even edible."

"You have to use a knife."

"Good to know. Next time I'll use a knife." We embrace.

Later in the week, Adnan gives the big diamond ring to his house manager, Frank, the asshole who terrorized me in the African brush. I feel betrayed, stabbed in the chest. Maybe that ring didn't mean that much to him anyway.

Our time in Kenya is totally hedonistic—sex, food, swim, safari, repeat. Even though AK has explained his pleasure wife situation, I don't realize that Sabine, the girl who had joined us in Spain, is also his pleasure wife. When I look back after the fact, I understand why she was so cold toward me.

I want to stay in Kenya and go on to the Canary Islands with Adnan, but I have promised to be a bridesmaid in my friend's wed-ding in California. Adnan's pilot takes me from the ranch to the airport in Nairobi in a small prop plane. We hit a terrible storm and lightning strikes all around us. The plane drops hundreds of feet at a time. I'm terrified, but I surrender to the storm, trusting and hoping something bigger has got the situation under control.

As the pilot lands the plane at the Nairobi airport, he says, "We made it! I didn't want to tell you, but that was the worst storm I've ever flown through."

I proceed into the terminal, still shocked that we survived.

Cheating death makes me ask the bigger questions of life: Why was I spared? What is the purpose of my life?

The Nairobi airport is the absolute opposite of my time with Adnan. The poverty of Africa is everywhere. Sad, gaunt faces, dirty rags for clothes, duct-taped boxes instead of suitcases. I am firmly back in reality—the words "disturbing," "depressing," and "confusing" don't begin to scratch the surface of my thoughts. After three hours in this tragic terminal, I board a crowded, smelly, eleven-hour flight to Paris.

I rush to my apartment to pack a few things and let Madame know I'll be gone for about a week. I stop by my new agency to the news I'm booked for three weeks of magazine editorial in Milan, Italy, right after the wedding. Then, it's off to Charles de Gaulle and another eleven-hour flight to Los Angeles.

On the long flight, I reflect on the changes in my life over the past eight months. I'm finally making it as a model, but don't care as much about it as I thought. I hated Paris at first, but now I love it—it's my new home. I left a bad relationship with Jack, and am in a great new one with Adnan. I lost some friends I grew up with, but have a lot of new ones. I used to be blind to the games of modeling, but now maybe I know a little too much.

I've also fulfilled my lifelong dream of going to Africa. I've swum new oceans and seas. I've gone without food, and I've been fed too much. I've been poor, and lived in wealth. I've worn flea market clothes, and handmade Paris Couture.

My Karin Models composite

TOKYO OR MILAN?

Halloween 1980, Downey, California

After customs at LAX, I make it just in time for Penny's rehearsal dinner at the Pleasant Peasant, a French restaurant in Downey. It's a nice transition to speak French with the owners of the restaurant, in my hometown. Since it's October 31, after dinner I meet friends at a Halloween, backyard keg party—just like old times.

In the morning, I join Penny and the bridesmaids in the bridal room of her church. These are what I considered conservative and rich North Downey girls, not South Downey, like me. They giggle nervously, undressing in front of one another like it is such a big deal to strip down to their bras, long slips, pantyhose, and grandma panties, while I'm fresh from strolling topless at the Indian Ocean. All these girls are from protective, loving families who shelter them from the world. I'm here for only one reason: Penny.

After the ceremony, when the wedding photographer takes photos, the scene is so surreal that I have to actually get into character. Young guys in rent-a-tuxes pose with us, in our long, floral, chiffon dresses and with baby's breath and plum-colored roses in our hair, the whole banana. It is a total juxtaposition to my life. Not just life with Adnan, but my entire life.

The next week, I go check in with Wilhelmina. I haven't had contact with them since my brief visit in August, and they assume I am still in Paris. Steve, my favorite booker, is on the phone, so I hide behind him till he hangs up. I put my hands over his eyes and he spins his chair around. "Oh my God, Jill! What are you doing here?" He jumps up to hug me.

"Just visiting. I'm going back to Paris soon, then Italy."

"You should stay, we need you here. It's so busy I could book you right now."

"I can't. I'm booked in Italy next week." As I hear the words come out, I feel a surprising tinge of doubt about my plans. "But you know, I'm not really sure how I feel about it now," I say.

"What do you mean?" he says.

"I don't know. It's great editorial, but I'm so tired of getting paid shit. I wouldn't mind making some money."

"Well, not to tempt you, but your new rate here is two hundred dollars an hour, twelve hundred a day, and of course, lingerie and swimwear is double. Just something to think about." Steve smiles, while I calculate. "If you want to make money fast, though, you should go to Japan. American girls are hot now and the pay's insane—twenty-five to thirty-five thousand a month, but you work twenty-four-seven. You'll barely sleep."

I picture myself modeling at night in a Tokyo high-rise. Getting lost in a foreign country sounds good, the adventure is intriguing, and if I had fifty grand in the bank, I could travel with Adnan without the embarrassing issue of who's paying for my plane tickets. "Know what? Let's do it. I'd love to go to Japan."

"Absolutely. But in the meantime, let's book you here. Everybody's gonna want to hire you fresh from Paris, you know."

"Yes, please!" I say. He is right. *Teen* magazine books me, and *New York Apparel News* wants me to shoot their cover.

◆

It's just my first week home, but I'm stir-crazy at night and want to go out dancing at clubs! I call Nicole, my friend since we were twelve.

"Hi, Nicole, I'm just back from Paris. Would you want to go out dancing with me?"

"Sure, how about now?" she says.

"Yes! I'll come get you!"

I drive to her house, not far from mine, and visit with Nicole and her parents in their living room. Her house feels so homey. Her parents are older than mine. Her dad is silver-haired, tall, and thin, and Hungarian, like my family. Her mom is buxom, dresses conservatively, and is always either smiling, laughing, or nagging at Nicole.

"Now, you girls don't stay out too late tonight. And watch out for weirdos. You know, Nicole, strange men hang out at nightclubs. And don't drink too much."

"Yes, Mom, I know. I'll be careful," Nicole says.

It is clearly loving nagging, not bitchy nagging. Nicole's dad says, "Nicole, do what your mother tells you."

"Dad, I'm twenty-one! I can take care of myself."

"Your mother's right. You girls be careful out there," he says.

It's so sweet. I can tell they love her. We go to her bedroom to get her purse, and I see framed family photos lining the hallway floor to ceiling—baby pictures, her parents' wedding photo, high school portraits, her brother's football newspaper clippings, her sister's prom picture, and all of their graduation photos with the hats and diplomas.

This is the opposite of my house with the embarrassing and massive wall of nudes in our den. I feel so jealous. I want a nagging, loving mom who proudly displays my achievements on the wall. I feel shame. I feel dirty, less than Nicole, not good enough.

We meet up with a group of her California State University–Long Beach friends at Bobby McGee's in Long Beach. She introduces me to Matt, a tall, handsome, half-Mexican, half-Irish guy. He's adorable. There must have been ten in our group. We all dance till closing time to the B-52s, the Clash, the Ramones, the Go-Go's, and A Flock of Seagulls.

On another night with Nicole, I run into my ex-boyfriend Jack at the Red Onion. The first time I see him, I am so shaken, my knees actually buckle. I want to surrender to him and our lust, but my head screams no! Each time I bump into him, my heart pounds out of my chest a little less, until I finally get over him for good. I had run away from our relationship by going to Paris and hadn't taken time to grieve.

Nicole makes my life fun. It's actually nice to be back in California. Everywhere I go I run into old friends. With work during the day and dancing at night, Thanksgiving, Christmas, and New Year's pass in a flash. No one, however, besides Nicole, knows the real details of my private life.

I write to Madame in Paris to let her know that I won't be returning quite yet. I feel conflicted about putting off the Italian editorial, but they say they can rebook after Japan. I want cash in the bank and another adventure. I sign a contract with Paul Rose, my Japanese agent, and am set to leave in February.

I write letters to Adnan, addressed to his mansion in Paris, to let him know my plans and I jump back into work in Hollywood while I wait for February to roll around. Since Wilhelmina's clients want to hire a model fresh from Paris, I'm working a lot.

Plus my old clients in the swimwear industry need me for fittings. Stick me in a sewing factory and I'm one happy girl.

Hello? Los Angeles

99-CENT SHRIMP COCKTAIL

Winter 1981, Las Vegas

Japan in February approaches fast, and with unexpected anxiety. Something doesn't feel right. All I can think about is Adnan. Why hasn't he reached out to me? I write letters telling him where I am, but he doesn't get back to me. I'm used to guys pursuing me like crazy. I don't get it.

Living on opposite sides of the world isn't helping, and Japan would be farther. I hate going back on my word, but with a heavy heart, I cancel Japan. I will return to Paris and Italy to be close to Adnan. But just before I buy my ticket, he calls.

"Jill, is this you?" he says in his playful Buddha voice.

"Adnan? Where are you?" I say, shocked and slightly angry.

"I'm very close to you," he teases.

"Where?"

"I'm in Las Vegas."

"No. I can't believe it!"

"Come see me. I'll send you a plane ticket."

My heart jumps. I feel so relieved our love isn't just a crazy fantasy in my mind!

Growing up, I spent several weeks a year in Vegas visiting my

grandparents. I thought I knew it well, but I am about to see another side. Because there's regular Vegas, and then there's Adnan's
Vegas. The one I know is a tacky tourist town filled with casinos;
disgustingly large all-you-can-eat buffets; and supersize 99-cent
shrimp cocktails.

Adnan's Vegas is a hedonistic rush of glamour and consumption,
secret dining rooms, private gambling rooms, bulletproof limos, private planes, cocaine, nine-course feasts, diamonds, and, of course,
Paris Couture.

I drop my car at LAX's Parking Lot C, and in forty-five minutes I'm in Vegas. It's a strange flight, visually. You take off in Los
Angeles, fly out over the ocean, and make a U-turn. Then you pass
over smog-filled, brown, flat urban sprawl. You blow by a sliver of
green trees on the San Bernardino Mountains, and then the earth
becomes instantly flat again; a barren desert of white salt beds and
sand, and clear blue skies. The Las Vegas Strip appears in the middle of the huge sandpit, its main vein branching into the desert on
either side. When I was little, we used to drive five hours through
the hot desert to get here. Now it takes under an hour.

Adnan stays at a private compound at the Sands Hotel, given to
him by Howard Hughes, the aircraft billionaire who owns the hotel.
(The Venetian stands there today.) Adnan's compound is behind the
main hotel, a series of one-story cottages and suites.

Someone from the front desk shows me to my suite. The first
thing I see is a collection of couture dresses hanging from the closet
doors and draped on the bed. I drop my bags to take a closer look.
Yes, Dior, Chanel, Valentino, and Givenchy are all here.

I hear a knock at the door and I open it to a hairy, muscular man
with a massage table under his arm.

"I'm here for your massage, miss."

"But I didn't ask for . . . oh, okay, come in." I strip down and get
on the table. I'm Jell-O when he's done.

The phone rings. "Hello?"

"Jill, is it you?"

"Yes, Adnan. It's me!" I'm freaking out.

"So we can see each other! It's been so long!" He sounds happy too.

"Oh my God, I can't believe you're here in Las Vegas! Where are you?"

"In my suite. I'll have Keith come get you."

Keith comes right over. We hug and kiss cheeks. I always want to be closer with Keith, but he's so professional and guarded. He wears a suit, even in this heat.

"Jill, how are you? Long time no see." He smiles.

"I'm good. It's so good to see you. How've you been?" I ask.

"Good, good, did you see the dresses I picked out for you?" He motions toward the bed.

"My God, they're beautiful!" I touch the beading, velvet, and lace. "Isn't this too much? Are they all for me?"

He nods. "You're gonna need them for all the dinner parties you'll be going to."

"Well, okay, when you put it that way." I raise my eyebrows, looking up at him. Keith is very tall.

"Come on, I'll take you to AK."

The Sands compound isn't as impressive as Adnan's other houses. It's outdated and original to the sixties, when Howard Hughes stayed here. It looks like Elvis's Graceland. His private suite at the Sands is the only part that has been updated with marble floors and modern furniture.

Adnan walks in, smiling, in his usual white *thaub*, arms spread out. "How are you, darling?" We hug and kiss.

"I'm good." Ahhh . . . the relief I feel in his arms. I relax instantly.

"What have you been doing in California for so long?"

"I've been working, you know."

"You know that business goes nowhere. Why don't you stop and travel with me? We could have been together all this time. I thought you were returning to Paris." He leads me to his adjoining bedroom.

"So did I. I almost went to Japan, but had a gut feeling I shouldn't. Maybe I wasn't supposed to go, because I was supposed to see you here."

"I'm so glad you listened to your intuition, because now we're together again." He hugs me.

He made his views on modeling clear many times. He wanted me to give it up so I could travel with him. There is no way I could let go of my safety net of an income and a career. What if things didn't work out with us? I'd have to start all over again from square one. I was too afraid to depend on a man for financial security.

"Did you receive my letters?" I ask.

"Yes, of course."

"But you never wrote me back." I scowl.

"I'm not good about writing letters, but I called you."

"Almost three months later! Did you really read them?"

"You don't believe me?" He smiles, sensing a challenge.

"No. I don't. Then what did they say?" I cock my head.

He goes into a long recitation, declaring everything I had said in detail, even describing the stationery. I'm stunned. "I'm right, aren't I?" He laughs. When I dispute a few facts, he says, "Would you like to bet?" and picks up the phone, calling Paris and requesting copies to be faxed immediately. "You'll see. My memory is never wrong."

Minutes later, the faxes start spitting out from the machine and to my horror, he reads them out loud. Listening to my own corny love letters is excruciating. He's right about every detail; he smiles and pushes me onto the bed. We make love because I cannot resist him.

As I snuggle into his neck, he repeats, "Why do you have to work? Why can't you be with me, and travel with me? Why can't you be like other girls and use your spare time to take tennis or dance lessons?"

"I can't imagine doing that! I need to work! I like working. I'd go crazy just taking tennis lessons. That's not me." Since I was a teen, I had wanted to move out from my parents' house and be free. How could I give up on my dream of freedom and independence? How would I spend my days? Lounging on a ship? Napping in a hotel room? Playing tennis? I have way too much energy for that. Resting and being pampered while on vacation is one thing, but I can't imagine living on permanent vacation at twenty-one years old.

"Okay then, why don't you go and take a nap and meet me here for dinner at eight?"

I return to my suite to find the bathroom stocked with Moroccan mint bubble bath, vanilla candles, and Adnan's favorite soap: African Black Mango. On the dressing counter is a tub of Queen Bee cream that he loves, made from beeswax and honey. I'm back in pure luxury.

I light every candle around the marble tub, pour the sweet mint liquid under the warm water, and relax into my private paradise. Warm and totally limp, I climb into bed and request a wake-up call. After a nap, I do my makeup and pull on stockings and shoes. I choose the black velvet-and-lace Dior dress for tonight and pull it from its hanger. It must weigh five pounds. I step in, zip it up backward, and twist it around the right way. It fits perfectly. I look in the full-length mirror. This dress is so beautiful—I can't believe it's on me.

I meet Dominic, Ines, and Bob Shaheen in AK's salon, along with several other new people. I'm so excited to see Dominic and Ines again. I missed them so much after spending all those weeks in Spain and Africa together. Dominic introduces me to everyone, and we toast Adnan as he walks in.

We are driven in limos to the back entrance of the MGM Grand and ushered to a secret dining room. Once again, a long table glows with candles and sparkles with crystal. Always a gentleman, Adnan tucks me into my chair and goes to sit across from me, but one seat to the right.

Moments later, a woman walks in looking like a young queen. She is escorted to the chair next to mine, directly across from

Adnan. Her dress is full length, made of purple velvet and red silk, which makes her look like a real-life Disney princess. Her long black hair falls in curls around her shoulders. Heavy eyeliner is drawn around her blue eyes, and her lips are red. She looks about thirty-five. At twenty-one, I feel like a child next to her. (In reality, she is only twenty-eight.)

Adnan introduces us. "Jill, this is Lamia. Lamia, meet Jill." We shake hands and then she graciously ignores me. She makes me so nervous. I want to connect with her, girl to girl, but she's not interested in getting to know me. She knows why I'm here.

And here I am, thinking I'm part of a big happy family. Lamia is Adnan's only legal wife after his divorce from Soraya. Ines had told me about her while we were in Spain, saying her name was Laura, she was Italian, and she had known Adnan since she was seventeen. Ines had pointed out old photos of her playing tennis at the house when we were in Spain. If they were involved since she was seventeen, then maybe it was Adnan who left the marriage first.

I find it hard to stop staring at her. Her massive emerald-cut solitaire diamond ring covers the whole area between the knuckle of her ring finger and her hand. I try to focus on not screwing up my table manners, instead of looking at her royal dress, ring, and makeup. She even smells good.

After dinner, Adnan and I hole up in his bedroom for days. His chefs intermittently bring food and champagne to the lush, quiet room, where we make love, laugh, talk, read, and sleep. We share his supply of cocaine, and I'm safe again with him in paradise.

+

Dominic and Ines invite me to dinner. "And Adnan too?" I ask.

"No, just the three of us. We'll pick you up at eight."

They are the ones who had welcomed me into this world, and I trust them one hundred percent. Dominic arrives in a suit, with Ines dressed in ruffled white taffeta, dripping in gold and diamonds. I wear the Dior and Ungaro skirt and blouse Adnan gave me in Paris when my zipper broke.

We sit down for dinner at Caesars Palace, when Dominic starts in, "Jill, you're such a lovely, intelligent girl, but that's not why we're here. We're here to teach you formal European table etiquette." Shame and humiliation rush through me. What was I doing wrong?

Ines adds, "You'll thank us later, darling." Then, in a serious tone, she says, "You'll be attending important business dinners with politicians and princes from all over the world, and I'm not sure you know how to hold a fork and knife properly." She unfolds her napkin into her lap. "See, Jill, you eat like an American. We'll teach you to eat like a proper European."

I remember back to my confusion over the silverware at our first dinner on Adnan's yacht, and every single one since. Which fork was for which course?

Ines continues, "First of all, when you sit in your chair, you must sit with your back completely straight. Never lean on the back of your chair and absolutely no leaning on the table." I had never heard of such a thing as not using the back of a chair.

Dominic says, "Ines and I noticed you slouching last night, and sometimes you lean with your elbows on the table." My heart drops into my stomach. I nod, blue-collar girl from Downey.

Ines continues, "When the gentleman pulls your chair out, you sit yet lift yourself up a bit so he can push your chair in. Then, you unfold your napkin, placing it in your lap. Notice your glasses are on the right. We drink champagne first, and then white wine with the first course, red with the second. You will always be poured both still water and water with bubbles." I think, *So that's how it works*. "Start with your outermost fork and knife and work your way inward. The fork is held in your left hand, upside down with your index finger on top."

"But I'm right-handed," I counter.

"Your knife is held in your right hand." She demonstrates. "Cut a very small piece and slide it up the back of the fork using your knife. Rest the knife at the edge of your plate. Place the bite into your mouth with the fork upside down." This part's tricky, and takes me a while to master.

As our meal is served, they continue demonstrating the proper use of the salad fork, the fish fork and knife, the dessert fork and spoon, and the café spoon. I don't talk. I sit up straight, nod, and try to memorize these rules. Knowing they're watching me and my manners, I think back to my humble beginnings in Downey, where we didn't have a fish fork or a fish knife. I still have no idea what Dominic does for a living, but evidently I'm one of his responsibilities.

It doesn't dawn on me until years later that I was in a modern-day harem. It took me years to admit. I already had enough shame shoved upon me by anyone I told about Adnan. My friends were troubled enough about the fact that he was twenty-four years older than me. Whenever I tried to explain the situation to friends, they'd say, "So, you were in a harem?" I'd respond, "No! It isn't a harem. Are you thinking it's like the movies with a bunch of girls lying around on velvet pillows in belly-dancing outfits?" Admitting it was a harem would have added yet another, even worse layer of scandal and humiliation, and I wasn't able to be honest with myself about that.

I was always unconventional enough without adding a harem, so I tried to focus on our love and relationship—not the fact that it was a harem with multiple wives. I always defended the arrangement with Adnan because he was honest with me about it from the beginning.

Still, all harems, from the beginning of time, have fierce competition between the women. This was no different. I suffered occasional hurt and jealousy, and all of us women kept an eye on one another, but as long as I was his favorite, everything was fine in my world.

I'll never forget when Adnan came into my suite in the middle of the night and set a box on my bedside table and kissed my head. I wake up and turn to him. When he sees me, he whispers, "Oh, I have the wrong room. Sorry, go back to sleep. Keep the gift," and leaves. Before I can respond though, he is gone. Then, it hits me hard. My heart drops into my stomach. He thought I was another girl. I turn on the light and pick up the box.

There is no joy opening a gift not meant for you. Inside is a delicate, gray suede envelope, and inside that is an eighteen-carat solid gold necklace, curved to the shape of a woman's neck like a treasure from King Tut's tomb. I picture the two of them making love, and my heart physically aches. Doubt sinks in, and I am not sure I can handle this after all.

A day or two later, Adnan takes me on a date, alone, to a Japanese restaurant at Caesars. He may have been trying to make sure I wasn't angry. His limo driver takes us, and his bodyguard follows us into the restaurant. I think he reserved the entire restaurant because it is completely empty. It has a tropical jungle theme with palm trees, a waterfall, and even a river and bridge.

After we order, he excuses himself, saying he left something in the car. When he returns, there is white powder around his nose. If he is that tired, I think, we shouldn't have come out in the first place. Once the coke kicks in, he is his animated, engaging self again.

When he notices my goose bumps from the cold air-conditioning on my bare shoulders, he says, "Come on, come with me!"

I follow him out into the adjacent shops and he pulls me into a fur-coat store. "Pick one," he says. They're so beautiful and soft. I don't think about the cruelty involved and choose a hip-length white fox. The lining is white silk satin, and the whole thing is soft and warm. We don't return to our food; instead, we go gambling.

Adnan loves to gamble, and we always play at private gaming rooms where he can gamble big money. (He is known as a "whale," one of the largest gamblers in the world.) We sit at the 21 Table, gambling stacks and stacks of $10,000 chips. We're both competitive, so we try to beat not only the dealer, but each other. He lets me play with the $10K chips too. He must have lost $300,000 in one sitting, but he's not bothered in the least. Afterward, we return to his suite and his bed. He succeeds temporarily at getting my mind off his mistaking me for another woman.

I need to return to Los Angeles for work, but promise Adnan I'll come back as soon as I can. Dominic makes my flight arrangements, and I am transported back into the real world. I fly commercial to LAX and take the shuttle bus to Long Term Parking Lot C, to my light-green 1970 Ford Fairlane 500. Cruising down the 405 Freeway with all the windows down, I blast Queen on the stereo, shedding all the layers of Vegas life with Adnan. As I pull into my parents' driveway, my hair is blown in a thousand different directions, and every trace of Vegas is packed tightly away.

Adnan and me in Nairobi, Kenya, 1980

THE SANDS

Las Vegas, Nevada

The flight into the desert is my new weekly routine. Taxis adorned with showgirls swirl around the Vegas McCarran airport. The marquees at Caesars Palace, the MGM, and the Hilton spell out in bold letters—Cher, Tom Jones, Liberace, and Wayne Newton.

Sometimes, I go visit my grandparents straight from the airport. They live in a suburb three miles from the Strip. The limo driver always says, "Sure you know where you're goin'?" As we pull up to the chain-link fence that surrounds their tiny, pastel-pink home, he repeats, "Sure she lives here? Should I wait, or you wanna call me when you're done?" I tell him to leave because the neighbors are already staring at the limo. He's always surprised when I tip him, saying, "You know, all those high rollers? They don't tip me. They act so rich, but they don't tip."

I have happy memories of my grandparents' house. As a kid, my sister and I stayed with Nano and Grampy for several weeks every summer. The rooms of Nano's home are painted in various shades of pastel from mint green to pink, baby blue, and yellow.

Nano's hugs and kisses were the only affection I got growing up.

She always tucked me into bed saying, "Good night, honey, God love her." It was so comforting.

My sister, Nano, and I would bake cakes, eat bologna sandwiches with soft Wonder Bread and mayo, and play cards at the kitchen table late into the night. Nano's constant giggling was the icing on the cake. Grampy went to bed early, and the three of us would laugh to tears at his loud, funny-sounding snoring. Nano would take me to the supermarket across from Fletcher Jones's car lot, where I'd watch the old ladies play the slot machines that ran the length of the store windows by the checkout stands.

The old women would sit, decked out in their polyester ensembles and wigs, chain-smoking. They'd pull the black ball on the slot machine handles, balancing red-and-white cardboard buckets of nickels on their laps.

After dusk, when the outdoor temperature cooled, we would venture outside, away from the air-conditioning. Cicadas buzzed and bats flew around. At dark, we'd lie on the driveway, watching stars for hours. The desert was so dark that the stars lit up the night sky. My sister always spotted shooting stars.

These days, Nano's house is much quieter. Grampy's stroke paralyzed him and he is in a wheelchair. Nano never complains about caring for him. Since the stroke, Grampy can't control his emotions, and just the sight of me coming in the door makes him cry. Cooking, playing cards, and pushing Grampy through the mall are our simple pleasures. Their home is my sanctuary in the middle of the beautiful Nevada desert.

✦

Adnan's bed is the one place where we both can escape the stress of the world. He has two bedrooms at the Sands, and we spend most of our time in the quietest, most private one. It is also the tackiest, because it hasn't been remodeled since the Howard Hughes days, a relic of sixties decor, complete with a gilt framed mirror on the ceiling above the bed. The one unifying thing is the ever-present scent of vanilla candles.

We lie in bed, drinking champagne, talking, and laughing, while his staff tiptoes in with silver platters overflowing with seafood and fruit. Day bleeds into night as we indulge in each other.

Cocaine, the white powder I once feared, has now become a mainstay, heightening our emotional and intellectual connection. Adnan pours a pile of coke on my breast and inhales it from a shiny silver tube. "So Jill, tell me again about your lesbian lover."

"I told you I never had a lesbian lover!" I laugh.

He dabs cocaine on my vagina, licks it off. "Okay then, tell me again about how you lost your virginity."

"Do you really want to talk about that now? You're crazy!"

He busts up laughing. "No, I really don't want to hear about that. You're right."

"What about you and Lamia?" My vagina is numb.

"I'm the one who should be jealous."

"Lamia? She's . . ."

He draws the shape of a square on the sheet with his fingertips. "You're more fun."

"Thank you." I dip a strawberry in hot fudge and feed it to him.

While he feeds me lobster and shrimp, he asks me again how many lovers I've had and how old I was the first time. I tell him again that my only lover was Jack, and that I was eighteen when it began. I still don't mention Gerald.

He loves playing head games, tricking me, and making bets like, "Do you know how many pyramids are in Egypt? If you're right, I'll give you five thousand dollars. But if I'm right, you pay me five thousand."

I'd interrupt, "I can't afford to lose that much!"

"Okay, two hundred dollars." We have a deal. His brain is on fire. He has a crazy amount of mental energy. Sometimes, when I first arrive, I forget how intense he is until he sideswipes me with a confusing, sometimes sarcastic, tricky comment. But I love bantering with him.

We debate everything from world history and archeology, to health, fashion, and religion. There are always books around the bed, and we read poetry and Shakespeare to each other. I feel safe with him, so much so that when we are apart, I picture his face in my mind to feel calm. He must feel safe with me too because he allows himself to fall apart in front of me, sometimes crying in my lap.

I'm not here for power, but knowing that the wealthiest man in the world is in love with me is a powerful feeling. If I were the manipulative type, I could see how a woman would think, *He bows to me in bed and he's wealthy and powerful. So how powerful does that make me? If I can control him in bed, then I must have tremendous power.*

Looking back, I wonder . . . he must have thought I was a strange girl. I must have been the only person he knew who wasn't after his money. Yet, he always repeated to me, "Stay with me—you'll be the richest girl in the world."

His currency of love, Paris, 1980

THE CURRENCY OF LOVE

"Jill, I need to explain the seating at our dinners. There's a specific structure to it. The wife who's been with me the longest always sits directly across from me." We're lying in bed in the jazzy Howard Hughes suite.

"You mean way across at the other end of the table?" I ask. "Wouldn't you want to sit next to her?" This makes no sense.

"Yes, directly across, either lengthwise or in the middle," he says, logically.

"Well, I like sitting close to you." *Why would the closest one emotionally be the farthest away?* I flash back to Sabine in Kenya, always sitting at the opposite end of the long table from him. I hadn't known they were involved, but was putting it together. "So Sabine, in Kenya, was she your number one wife?"

"Yes, because Lamia wasn't there. Lamia is my only legal wife and has seniority. Whichever wife is present and has the most seniority will always be across from me."

"So, Sabine is a pleasure wife?" I want to be clear.

"Yes, she is."

In my mind, all men behave badly—at least Adnan is up front and honest about it. Maybe this is the perfect arrangement? If I don't expect monogamy, then I can't be disappointed.

"Have you met Camille?" he asks.

"I saw her a couple times with Ines at Caesars." I flash to an image of her in red leather pants, stilettos, and a red-fox-fur coat, her long, wavy, mane of golden-brown hair draping everywhere.

"I'll tell you a story. She was living in an apartment I bought her on the Île Saint-Louis in Paris."

"That must have been nice," I say.

"Yes, but I had a feeling she was lying to me."

"About what?"

"About a man she was seeing. She kept telling me they were just friends. You know what I did?"

"What?" I ask.

"I bugged her apartment and recorded her having sex with him—which would have been okay if she hadn't lied about it. I confronted her, and she lied again. So I took out the recorder and pressed Play."

"Oh my god."

"I can't stand lies."

We never run out of things to talk about. One time he blurts out, "I just ordered five AWACS for Saudi Arabia." (Congress had just passed a bill allowing the US to sell AWACS to Saudi Arabia.)

"What did you say?" I ask.

"AWACS. It stands for 'Airborne Warning and Control System.' They're like reconnaissance planes—air defense equipment," he explains. "It's a totally new technology with a rotating radar dome on top."

"Oh, so you buy military equipment?" I ask.

"I sell it," he says, and sits up leaning into me, very excited about the topic. "If you want to make a lot of money, Jill, go into sales. There's no limit to what you can make on commissions."

My imagination is big, but I never would have thought he was referring to a commission on an $8.5 billion deal.

"Doesn't selling military equipment promote war?" I ask.

"All countries have the right to protect themselves," he responds, which sounds logical.

"I guess you're right." I go back to reading Shakespeare to him.

"Want to know how I get the advantage in my business deals?" he asks.

"Yeah, sure."

He gets even more animated. "I use their ego. I have businessmen picked up in a limo and brought to the airport, where they board my DC-8. My plane is stocked with girls, champagne, and cocaine. The girls work for me, the coke inflates their egos, and by the time they meet with me, they're feeling so sure of themselves that they're easy to play."

He tells me that he has the girls brief him with any insights before the meetings, and that he uses this strategy on his boat too. "In the beginning of our meeting, as they sit down, I put extra pillows behind them, like I'm being a good host, but really I'm pushing them off balance and making them uncomfortable. It's all a game to gain the advantage over your opponent."

"Wow, does it work?" I say, amazed, picturing these scenes in my head.

"Of course. Men always talk after sex." Adnan talks a lot after sex too, but I'm not trying to steal his secrets.

◆

I take my relationship with AK seriously, yet I think Lamia probably sees me as just another girl passing through. When I run into her around the grounds of the Sands, I try to strike up a conversation, but she's not interested in being my friend. It's awkward.

He prefers sex with me, yet she has known him longer. She looks like Priscilla Presley in the sixties, when she married Elvis: big black bouffant, white trousers, bright-patterned blouses, and dripping in diamonds. When I ask if I can see her earrings, she leans over with a manicured finger behind one of them. The sparkling cluster is two inches long, shaped like a leaf, and encrusted with huge diamonds. I am starting to understand that these extravagant gifts are a reflection of his love, as well as physical evidence of his commitment.

Big jewels—I think that I'd never be comfortable settling for that as the currency of his love. Yet, it isn't long before I crave them.

Back in bed, he says, "I want to share something with you. Lamia and I have a young son. In my culture, we don't have baby showers when the mother is pregnant and uncomfortable. We have them when the child turns one year. Our son, Ali, is one now, and I'd like you to come to his party on Saturday. Will you?"

"Of course, I'd love to." I act happy, but feel confused. I had no idea they had a baby. Maybe they'd hit that ten-year mark? I wonder if I'll want to have a baby with him too in ten years?

"Do you still make love with her?" I ask.

"Not anymore. I like making love with you."

I feel flattered but awkward. Ines had made Lamia sound like she was a daughter to him. Maybe they were like platonic family members now. He did say his sperm was frozen in a bank, so she must have been artificially inseminated. Whatever the truth, I don't care about his sperm. I need to know I hold his heart.

I go to the mall to look for a baby present. What do you buy the baby who literally has everything? And what should I wear? I settle on a stuffed animal and blue satin blanket for baby Ali, and a conservative lavender floral dress for myself.

A baby shower fit for a prince is all set up in a private suite. Flowers, balloons, dainty finger sandwiches and desserts, and champagne are arranged on long tables. There are men *and* women, not like the all-girl baby showers I had been to. I am the only pleasure wife. Lamia walks in looking glamorous (think Joan Collins in *Dynasty*) in a body-hugging, royal-blue velvet dress, matching pumps, and serious blue sapphire and diamond "queen jewelry," just like I saw in the catalogs at Adnan's Paris mansion.

Adnan arrives carrying little Ali, who has big brown eyes and long eyelashes just like his dad. As I remember, his outfit is also blue velvet, matching his mom's. Adnan and Ali play together on the floor while Nabila, his almost nineteen-year-old daughter, singles me out and says, "I hate my father's girlfriends. He spends too much time with you. I tried to hate you, but it's hard to hate you for some reason."

"I'm glad it's hard to hate me." I feel bad for her. How could he possibly spend enough time with her? She seems so angry. Who could blame her? She and I are just three years apart, but being her father's lover makes me feel a lot older. At that point, I excuse myself and go to ask the pastry chef how he creates all of the delicacies.

This is one strange family dynamic. I am infinitely more comfortable with Adnan, alone in his bed, where all things are equal.

◆

After the baby shower, I never see Lamia again, so at all the business dinners I now have the power position across from Adnan.

At one dinner, the table is dotted with foreign heads of state, some in Arab robes and headscarves, others in European suits. It is important to Adnan that I engage and amuse his guests. These conversations are some of the most stimulating I've ever had.

Next to Adnan sits an unbelievably beautiful girl, who reminds me of Grace Kelly. I'd never seen her before. "This is Milla. She's studying to be a doctor in Finland," Adnan announces proudly. How would he introduce me? *This is Jill, a model from Los Angeles?* I had no idea he dated college students. I am knocked off my throne and envious.

After the champagne and many courses, we all rise to kiss cheeks and say good night. Adnan and I leave in his silver bulletproof limo and return to the Sands.

I am welcomed by the comforting sight and smell of vanilla candles flickering next to his bed. He unzips my dress and helps me out of it. I undo his tie and unbutton his shirt. We stand between his bed and his dressing area on the cold marble floor in our bare feet. He is within an inch of my face, his olive skin glowing. I'm sure he feels my insecurity.

He takes my face in his hands and looks into my eyes saying, "I've been giving it some thought. I know you feel like you need to work. But if that's the case, you need an education. You need a serious career, Jill—not modeling." I stand silently, as tears run down my face. "You know I support college students all around the world. I started the school in Kenya. Everyone needs an education to pursue their passion."

I nod. "I know you're right. It's so hard for me to accept things from you. But this, I will accept." I am devastated and serious. I'm on the cusp of an enormous change and can't stop crying.

Adnan has just handed me the key to my future and I know it. After being out in the world modeling, instead of going to college like most of my friends, I know how important an education is. I don't want to wind up as an aging model with limited career choices, and I don't want to end up waitressing or doing some other mind-numbing job. I know now more than ever that an education is crucial. I know he is right.

He leads me to the bed and wipes my face with his hands. "Let me know what you decide, and find out how much it will cost. I'll pay for whatever you need." I am so emotional with him over every single thing. We make love while I cry. After saying good night, I walk the dim hallway to my room, where I sit at a desk, legs curled up on the chair, with the lamp on the lowest setting. It's four in the morning, but I'm too excited to sleep.

As I linger in the quiet darkness, I remember an event from years ago. During high school, I talked my parents into taking me to check out the Fashion Institute of Design and Merchandising (FIDM) in Los Angeles. I was convinced I needed to attend, but the tuition was $1,250 a year, five times more than community college. My parents said I could go after earning a Bachelor of Arts at a state school. But that meant four years of college before I could even start FIDM. My impatience and determination had to find a faster way, and my way was modeling. However, I had gotten so wrapped up in it that I had forgotten my original goal of going to FIDM.

I said out loud, "I want to go to fashion design school!" I picked up the phone, made a flight reservation, and jumped on the first plane out of Vegas.

Paris high-rise, 1980

FIDM

March 1981, Las Vegas to Los Angeles

I stare out the plane window at the pastel desert, nervously excited, my mind racing with possibilities. Paris has a fashion school, but if I go there I'll never return to live in the US and would miss my friends.

New York has FIT, the Fashion Institute of Technology, but I was afraid that I'd be tempted to dive back into modeling there—because modeling is like a drug and can be addicting. No joke. The highs are high and the lows are low. I return to the original reason I started modeling in the first place: to attend FIDM.

When I visited FIDM during high school, I remember it being in a tacky strip mall. Now, it occupies several floors of a high-rise in downtown. The woman in the admissions office tells me the tuition is $4,500 a year (which is expensive in 1981, but not for Adnan). The counselor says that the school puts on a big fashion show for the graduating students each year, where industry professionals come to watch. Some students are hired right out of school.

I return to Vegas to tell Adnan the news. He's in bed working when I rush in. "I found the school I want to go to! FIDM. It stands for the Fashion Institute of Design and Merchandising, and they teach fashion design, illustration, and patternmaking. It's perfect!" I'm hoping he'll share my enthusiasm.

Adnan puts his papers aside. "Come here, darling." He lifts the sheets. I step out of my boots and jump in. "This is such good news. And when you graduate, I can open a couture house for you in Paris if you'd like. Remember, I helped Kenzo."

"I figured out that I'll need about ten thousand dollars for the two-year Associates of Arts program, including books and supplies." Adnan goes to his safe at the foot of the bed and pulls out two large stacks of bills wrapped with paper bands.

"Here's twenty thousand dollars. This should cover you for a little while. No working while you're in school, okay? You need to focus on your studies. Now, do you need a car? Can I buy you a house near school?"

"No, no, this is too much already."

He gets back in bed. "You're going to need extra money for the things girls buy, like lipstick." He giggles.

I snuggle into his neck with my head on his shoulder and stroke his hairy chest through the opening of his *thaub*. "I can't believe you're doing this for me." Tears roll down my face onto him.

Later, when I return to my room, I look at the money: two large bundles of crisp one-hundred-dollar bills, each wrapped in a narrow paper belt. I count one hundred bills in each stack totaling $20,000. I had never seen this much cash in my life. Sunday night, as I dress for the airport, I shove the bundles of cash deep into the ankles of my black-and-red cowboy boots. Airport security would surely question me if they found them in my purse.

I'm so excited about getting an education that I go a little crazy and sign up for French lessons at the Alliance Française and Hwa Rang Do, South Korean martial arts, on top of FIDM. I also keep modeling, against Adnan's advice. At a shoot at Jim Britt's studio in Hollywood, I ask if anyone knows of a place that I could rent close to school. The advertising agent, Claire, says there's a vacancy below her, in Glendale, just a few minutes from downtown. I move in with my bed, a shipping crate I use as a coffee table, and two beach chairs. Coincidentally, Claire's father works for Adnan's brother, Essam Khashoggi.

School starts right away, in March. I pull into a parking lot on Figueroa and 9th and walk toward school. Homeless people are sprawled everywhere, still asleep. When I try to hand a twenty to a dreadlocked man sitting on a bench, he jumps at me, growling and shaking his box of Cheerios all over my head. This is my new neighborhood, for the next two years. Thankfully, I meet Benny Washington.

Every morning Benny stands in front of the Los Angeles Hilton, at 8th and Figueroa, across from FIDM, working as a doorman. He's a full-figured black man, about fifty years old, and he radiates peace and joy. I want what he has. Every morning, we stand in front of the hotel, talking: Benny in a brown hotel uniform, me in some wacky fashion student outfit.

Benny leads by example, not to be afraid of, or intimidated by, people living on the streets. Every morning as he is handed tips, he discreetly gives them to homeless men slogging by. They count on him. Benny is full of faith, compassion, and optimism. He knows the Bible, but never pushes it on me. He believes that people don't all get the same opportunities in life, and some suffer tragedy so great that their whole life is derailed. When mental illness and addiction are added, homelessness can be impossible to overcome.

The diversity at FIDM reflects the fashion business and the city itself. Students from all over the world—thick and thin, gay and straight, mostly young, but some old—come together to study fashion. My favorite: a petite, young Vietnamese man who struts the school halls in a shiny metallic suit, mirrored aviators, and a scarf fitted with wire inserts, making it look like it is blowing in the wind.

One buxom girl, with bright purple hair and tattoos, works as a stripper to pay for school. There are lots of students from Asia, who are so much fun once I break through their shyness. Together, we are a motley crew with a common passion.

Oh. I also make friends with Daisy, the girlfriend of a Colombian drug smuggler. I now have my own cocaine dealer.

Dior Couture, California, 1983

CHASING MY TAIL

Adnan moved from the Sands to the Dunes Hotel after renovating the entire penthouse, updating it with travertine marble and modern furnishings. He even built a pool on the roof. (The Dunes was blown up in 1993 to make way for billionaire Steve Wynn's Bellagio.)

The glass doors of the Dunes Hotel slide open, and I walk through a smoky haze of ringing bells and clanking coins. The armed guard calls the elevator when he sees me. My ears pop as I speed up to the penthouse in the box of tinted mirrors. The elevator slides open to another guard with his finger on the trigger of a machine gun. This is normal.

I head down the long hallway to my suite, across from Adnan's. I open the door and cross over the footbridge that arches over a small man-made stream in my foyer and see dozens of red roses on the coffee table. I smile, knowing he's been thinking about me. I toss my garment bag of couture dresses on the bed and walk to the window. My room is silent, and cold from the air-conditioning. Outside, the pastel desert is noiseless, still, and 105 degrees.

Adnan bursts through the door and mugs me with a bear hug. We fall onto my bed and wrestle around, laughing. He nuzzles my neck, inhaling, saying, "You smell so fresh even after traveling."

"It's just a thirty-minute flight!" I giggle as I climb on his belly, pushing my face into his. His eyes bring me instant peace. He can cure my anxiety with just a look. We kiss and make love, as always. I need him.

After, he leans over me, saying, "Why do you have to work? Stop working and travel with me."

"I'm in school now, remember?"

"Oh yes, I like that better. Just don't do any modeling, okay?"

"Okay, I won't work too much."

"You still want to be the wealthiest woman in the world, don't you?" He keeps asking this, and I never know what to say.

"I have to be able to take care of myself on my own."

"We'll continue this discussion later." He gets up, goes to my bathroom, and splashes around in the bidet. After a long pause, he says, "If you're so independent, why don't you take me out to lunch? Show me how normal people do it."

"What do you mean 'normal'?" I laugh.

"There's a place I've always wanted to go, no bodyguards. Want to?" He is as excited as a puppy.

"God yes, let's go."

His driver drops us in front of Caesars and we walk through the casino, toward the shops—no bodyguards. Adnan is always looking around, aware of who is around him. I don't understand why he could possibly be in danger.

We walk through the marbled halls of shops, giggling, when he stops in front of a self-serve cafeteria. "This is the place."

"What? Are you kidding me?"

"No, I'm not."

"Okay, let's go." So this is what a billionaire fantasizes about? Eating in a cafeteria like "normal" people? He studies the food behind the glass, not knowing what to do.

"Here." I hand him a tray. "You slide this along and put whatever you want on it."

He grabs one of almost everything. "Ooo, hot dogs, turkey, mashed potatoes with cranberry sauce. What's this?"

"Jell-O. You've never had Jell-O?" I laugh and grab another tray. "Don't you think that's enough?"

"No, we need dessert, let's get tiramisu. . . ." When we reach the cashier, we have three trays.

He doesn't let me pay, like we'd planned, and pulls out a wad of hundred-dollar bills—one for the food, two for the tip. He is used to multiple courses, so he tastes bites of each dish. After lunch we go couture dress shopping, and then back at the hotel he presents me with a watch he says I need because I'm in school, and a beautiful spinning ring. Every time my hand moves, the diamond and gold squares spin around in circles.

◆

As spring turns to summer, I fly back and forth to Vegas every weekend, carting all my homework along so I can work in my hotel room when I'm not with Adnan. It's more effort to travel while juggling school, but when I'm away from Adnan I miss him so much. He makes me feel so loved and calm and safe when I'm with him, that I do it anyway.

However, my life is becoming one hundred percent split in two. The contrasts between my lives in Vegas and Los Angeles are mind-boggling, with everybody pressuring me on either side to conform to their way of life.

When I lived in Paris, I was never judged for being with Adnan. I wasn't accountable to anyone. America is a totally different story. When my friends ask if I have a boyfriend, and I start explaining, they look at me in shock. Just the fact that he's forty-five and Saudi Arabian is enough to make them think I've lost it. Trying to explain the harem is totally not worth the effort. Adnan warns me not to tell anyone about our relationship, fearing someone will kidnap me and hold me for ransom. Adnan doesn't know any of my friends. I ask Nicole to come with me to Vegas so she can meet him, but she's afraid of his world and thinks the whole situation is insane. So, I keep talk about Adnan to a minimum. I can't blame her for thinking it's weird.

While my friends disapprove of my life with Adnan, he pressures me to give up my life and work to travel with him. He hates modeling, so I don't talk with him about work.

On a go-see in Hollywood I run into a model friend, Gwen, the girl whose photos I saw in Dominic and Ines's Paris apartment. When she spots my diamond rings, she asks, "Are those from Mohammed or Adnan Khashoggi?"

"Yeah, they're from Adnan. How'd you know?"

She jumps down my throat. "You can't wear those around! Everyone'll know what you're involved in!"

I feel a tinge of shame. "But why should anyone care what jewelry I wear?"

"You'll be blacklisted!" she says. She probably doesn't want anyone to know what she's involved in either.

Thankfully, my parents don't interrogate me. Alleen, on the other hand, totally freaks out. "Lambchop, you're gonna be kidnapped and held hostage on an island somewhere off the coast of goddamn Africa!" Her screenwriter husband happens to be working on a documentary in which a model picked up in Milan goes missing. "She's dead, Lambchop. She was sold to the Arabs! You need to get the hell away from these people, Jill."

She never called me Jill. No one seemed to approve of any part of my life except the part they were in. I fantasize about my simple life in Paris, where no one tells me what to do. I feel like I am the rope in a tug-of-war, with five different groups of people trying to pull me apart!

Teen *magazine, Hollywood, California*

HOLLYWOOD MIMICS REALITY

California's sunshine, sandy beaches, surf culture, and outdoor sports send the whole world an image of an "All-American California Cool." Television shows, movies, and commercials all capture the good life. From drinks like Coca-Cola, Pepsi, Sprite, Gatorade, and all the beer brands, to yogurt, cheese, sugary breakfast cereals, and granola bars, and of course makeup, hair products, and fashion, they all come to Los Angeles and Hollywood to shoot their ad campaigns and commercials.

Hollywood's job is to create the illusion that America is as perfect as a California sunset with beautiful, athletic, suntanned people enjoying paradise. Behind the scenes, though, it's a totally different story. I must look like an all-American girl, because I always land these jobs.

My Sprite commercial is shot in a Beverly Hills swimming pool. The athletic, clean-cut cast and I play water polo, guzzling Sprite to quench our thirst. The poor guy chosen for the close-up drank so much Sprite that he threw up between takes. They ended up using me in the final cut, and I only had to drink it twice.

Another commercial, for a German department store, is shot at Magic Mountain. The theme park is closed for filming and we ride every spinning, dizzying ride, from the huge roller coasters, to the tube that spins so fast that when the floor is lowered, you stick to the walls. We ride the big coasters over and over for multiple takes. Half of the actors are hurling, so as the day wears on, there are fewer and fewer of us to shoot.

I shoot a Japanese yogurt commercial in Santa Barbara with a model named Candy, whose image is on the cover of the *Candy-O* album by the Cars. She dated the Cars' drummer and was even friends with (and went clubbing with) Freddie Mercury! I was so jealous. We are hired for our figures and, as we find out later, our diving skills. Our agents asked us if we could dive into a swimming pool and of course we said yes. Who can't?

When the whole Japanese-speaking crew, Candy, and I get to Santa Barbara, the clients motion for us to dive off an Olympic high-diving board—thirty-three feet high—twirling as we go like Olympic divers, mimicking stirring a yogurt cup. This is communicated with hand motions because of course they don't speak English. I'm scared. I try to pretend I'm jumping off cliffs at the Colorado River so I can force myself to dive off a few times—just straight down, no flips, turns, or twists. The clients aren't happy. They want me spinning and twisting in the air like when you stir together that damn yogurt with the fruit on the bottom. Candy won't even jump at all. I don't think we will got paid for that one.

I audition for a French Coca-Cola commercial, which requires me to skimboard, something I have never done. I go to the notorious "Wedge" in Newport Beach, borrow a board from my friend Frankie, and try to learn. Right after a wave comes into shore, you are supposed to throw the thin, wooden, mini surfboard onto the smooth, wet sand, jump on the board while it's moving in the thin layer of water, and surf the sand, skimming along the wet surface.

After several runs, I start getting the hang of it and feel more confident, but on my last run, I forget to time the wave. It's during a big wave swell when body-boarders commonly die from broken necks at the Wedge. As I fly on the skimboard down the sand toward the water, I look up to see a massive wave about to crush me, so I spit the board out with my feet, avoiding the wave, and land in a pile of crushed shells that get embedded in my right thigh. With blood dripping down my leg, I limp through the sand to safety, picking out most of the shells while I'm still numb, before the pain sets in. Even though I can now skimboard, I am eliminated from the casting when the director sees the disgusting wound on my leg.

Then there is a commercial I will never forget—the German hair commercial. They need a model who can water-ski—now *that* I can do. I'm sure they envision a bikini-clad girl skiing off the coast of Malibu in the California sun with her hair blowing in the wind. This would fully represent the product and make everyone in Germany want to buy it. But, on the day of the shoot, it isn't sunny with blue skies—it is cold, dark, and stormy.

We board a fifty-foot yacht with a movie camera bolted to the deck. These Germans have obviously never water-skied. You need a speedboat, not a yacht. I try to explain, but they don't speak English. I figure I'll give it a go. How bad could it be?

We take off from Marina del Rey, bobbing in the huge-ass waves and freezing all the way to Malibu. The futile exercise of hair and makeup is performed on board, and I jump in the ocean with my skis and the rope. They take off slow, like a yacht does. When the rope is finally taut, I hold my breath while I am dragged underwater until the boat gets up enough speed to pull me out. An amateur skier could not do this. I'm not boasting—risking my life is ignorant. When I finally rise to the surface, skiing, I'm drenched. So they stop the boat and I sink back into the ocean. I tread water and wait an eternity for the yacht to turn around and find me.

Bobbing in the ocean is terrifying, the water is freezing, and the tiny life belt they give me is doing nearly nothing to keep me afloat. Huge waves crash on my head. I dive under them so they don't push me under. It's like bodysurfing in the middle of the ocean. I'm totally alone. I can't see land. I can't see the boat. It's just me, in the middle of the Pacific Ocean. I wonder if I'll drown.

I'm treading water, holding my skis, trying to stay calm because I'm thinking that sharks will smell my fear and eat me. Finally the big fucking yacht does its wide turn and somehow spots me in the six-foot swells.

When they finally appear, I climb back in, shaking. My lips are purple. I'm covered in goose bumps. They blow-dry my hair and style it all over again, telling me with hand language to not get it wet in the ocean. After repeating this futility three more times, I retire, shivering, to the captain's deck for the ride back. The captain is American—the only one on board who speaks English. He says, "I didn't want to tell you this, but we filmed the *Gilligan's Island* movie out here last week and we spotted a bunch of sharks." *Thanks for the warning, you asshole.*

We thrust over massive swells, up and down, being hit by waves that pour over the deck of the boat, drenching us, all the way back to Marina del Rey. I feel like this scene is the perfect illustration of what's going on in my life. I'm stranded in the middle of an ocean, churning with waves, waiting for help to arrive. Yet help is not coming. No one is going to step in and rescue me. No one is watching out for me. Everybody just takes what they want from me, without a care about how I'm doing—and I'm not doing well.

Mediterranean sea, summer 1980

QUESTION EVERYTHING

Billionaire wealth is a pain in the ass at least half the time. It's odd. The food is fresh, healthy, and prettier than a flower arrangement. The clothes are mostly handmade with quality, natural materials— no plastic, polyester, or vinyl. The views of the ocean, sea, or city lights are heavenly and can put anyone at ease. And having hired help leaves you so much time to think, prioritize what needs to be done, and decide what you want to do.

Yet as soon as you acclimate to all of this, it becomes the new normal, and expected. Then normal things, which used to be just fine, don't seem quite good enough. And the worst part is that all of this luxury can leave an unhealthy vacuum of space and time, where anxiety and guilt can thrive, creating a cesspool.

I never felt comfortable with the isolating feature extreme wealth and luxury has. The very rich live in an isolated bubble of champagne, chefs, intimate parties, maids, masseurs, hairstylists, skin care professionals, nannies, drivers, and private jets. They talk with one another about their hundred-year-old bottles of wine, how long their yacht is, or how they remodeled the interior of their private plane—something they can't discuss with others. Just like extremely beautiful people, extremely wealthy people are stared at like freaks.

Trust is a major issue for the wealthy, as many are paranoid about people's intentions, always wondering if others like them for who they are, or if they're after their money. Their need to protect their treasure and status causes them to be suspicious. Envy is ugly. People stare. You stare back, trying to remember what it was like to be so excited about winning fifty bucks at a slot machine, or drinking Mexican beer stored in your cheap Styrofoam cooler at the beach with your friends. Luckily for me, I lived in both worlds at the same time and got to compare.

I used to ask Adnan how he could justify being so rich, and what he does for the poor or war-torn areas of the world. "I load my airplanes with medicine and blankets and fly them to places in need," he'd say.

I'd push, "What about all your expensive cars, clothes, and houses? Don't you feel guilty about having so much?" Because I sure did.

"When I spend money, I create jobs. People who buy the finest things in the world spur growth in the economy and in each particular industry. When I order a special car, plane, or ship to be designed, this higher level of quality gives the whole industry something to strive for that elevates the quality, design, and engineering for products of all price ranges." He had me there.

"Oh, like couture houses. They set a standard for the entire world of fashion to emulate," I add. This made sense for the time being, but as time went on, I began to really question the idea of wealth and the unfairness of it.

The greatest gift that Adnan ever gave me was the understanding that wealth will never make me happier or more peaceful than I am without it. Beyond solving the problems of food, shelter, and health care, it doesn't change the way I feel inside. It doesn't automatically solve my problems or bring me inner peace, love, or joy. It only gives me short spurts of physical satisfaction that leave me hungry for more and make me obsess over filling the ever-widening gap in my heart. It makes me even more aware that something is missing.

◆

I try to believe in God, but I feel so ignorant about religion and think that without this knowledge, I can't know God. But I know there has to be more to life than what I can see with my eyes. I begin a whole new search.

Adnan and I have many deep conversations about God. I wish I knew more about world religion so I could contribute more than just questions. He has Islam, yet he exposes me to things besides the Quran, like his hypnotherapist, psychic, and holy man.

Adnan introduces me to Maria, his hypnotist, who was visiting the Sands Hotel. The first time I go under hypnosis she takes me on a subconscious journey of past-life exploration. It feels incredible to access my mind in this new way. I don't know if it is real, but it's intriguing to experience this parallel reality.

When I meet with his psychic, it's similar, except her insights are focused on the future, not the past. I wonder how these women can access time in a nonlinear fashion, seeing it all at once. Both women talk about spirits and angels that live among us. With my intense hunger for answers, I soon become obsessed with talking to them. I begin weekly appointments with the hypnotherapist, who lives in Los Angeles like me, and I call the psychic who lives in Vegas.

The dangerous part for me, though, is that I don't know how to live by faith, have patience, and trust in God. I want answers, and I want them now! I allow these sources of insight to become my god, and I turn their spiritual insights into my own anxious addiction. I'm so focused and obsessed with finding answers that it's unhealthy. I'm more confused than I was before, and my search for peace begins tearing me apart. It's not just the psychic and the hypnotist, though.

On set, filming a commercial for The Gap, I meet a girl who raves to me about her nutritionist in Hollywood, a Vietnamese man named Anthan. When I meet with him, I notice how full of peace he seems. I want to be filled with peace like he is, and I want to know how he achieved it. Over many months, we become close friends and on top of going out to eat together, he teaches me to cook Asian-style in his kitchen. During all of this eating and cooking, we talk about life. I learn that Anthan is a Buddhist and that he also reads palms.

I ask him so many spiritual questions, like "Why are we here? Who is God? Is there a God? Do you hear God speak to you? What is the purpose of life?" I go on and on. To aid me in my search, he takes me to the Bodhi Tree spiritual bookstore, where I buy armfuls of books on palm reading, astrology, I Ching, Carl Jung, Sufism, Buddhism, Hinduism, and a whole series on Egyptian mythology. I dive in hard, reading any chance I get. I'm searching so maniacally that peace is beyond my reach. My confusion level increases as I take in all of these varying and conflicting viewpoints.

At the same time, I continue to question wealth. Every religion I study seems to be against it. I feel guilty sharing Adnan's money and even wonder if I should give up all my possessions. I feel bad for all the people who have less than me and wonder if it's wrong to pursue fashion, since I am reading that material things are so empty. Should I become a monk and just pray and meditate? Why do some people suffer so badly from disease, hunger, war, and poverty and others don't? Why is the world so unfair? I question everything and drive myself crazy. Maybe the whole physical world is unimportant.

With Anthan's advice, I become a vegetarian. I cut out all meat, poultry, fish, and dairy. I have no idea how to be vegan in a healthy way. I don't know how to replace animal protein with vegan options. I become weak. At the same time, I'm working, taking an extra-heavy load at school, and continuing to travel to see Adnan.

I'm so hungry all the time, but I keep to my strict diet, punishing my body. Living strictly on fruit and vegetables sends my blood sugar on a roller coaster and I lose all of my muscle mass. My body feels mushy, even though I work out. All of this focus on what to eat and not eat becomes another nervous obsession and triggers a full-blown eating disorder. I've seen plenty of girls with this problem in Paris, but now the problem is mine. I starve myself, avoiding "bad food," then binge on ice cream and frozen carrot cake. I balloon up, gaining ten pounds, which would be okay if I weren't a swimsuit and fit model.

Everybody notices right away and keeps asking me over and over what's going on with my changing measurements. The pressure by clients for me to be thin stresses me out even more, and the more stressed I get, the more I obsess over food. I compulsively visit the hypnotherapist, who is able to calm me down while I am under hypnosis, but as soon as I come to, the panic returns. So I go home and call the psychic, circling around and around in a vicious cycle. It's ridiculous and so very sad. I keep my churning brain a secret. I've never been an anxious person, but I am one now.

I take everything to extremes. Everything I do, I do too much. If I go out dancing, I can't just go out one night a week, I go out three—fueled by cocaine. I am driven by nervous, restless anxiety. I don't know my limits. I don't know how to say no without feeling bad or guilty about it. As foolish and pathetic as it sounds, I don't even know that I'm not supposed to suffer. I think suffering is normal. I work to extremes, play to extremes, and try as hard as I can to push down my physical discomfort and mental anguish. I am determined to keep a lid on myself—instinctively afraid of a major blowout.

When Adnan asks if I want to meet "the holy man," I'm thrilled. I meet him in Adnan's Vegas penthouse, where he, Adnan, and I gather around the dining table, all wearing our white *thaubs*. It is late on a hot summer night. Outside the enormous floor-to-ceiling windows is a sky full of stars and a full moon. Brightly colored lights twinkle on the Strip down below us.

The holy man looks like Gandhi without the glasses, and somehow radiates peace and love. He doesn't speak English, so he communicates with hand motions. I can see why Adnan loves him so much. I want peace like he has. I wish I knew how he got it.

"He wants to tell you your future," Adnan says.

"Really? I'd love that." I feel honored as I try to act composed.

The holy man hands me a blank sheet of paper, motioning for me to crinkle it into a ball, which I do, and hand it back. Holding the crumpled ball in his hand, he carefully examines it. With Adnan interpreting, he says, "You will have three children. Far apart in age." That's a shock. Three children sounds like a lot, and why would they be spread apart? Could this be true? How could he know?

"Your marriage will end in divorce." *No!* I think. *There is no way I'm going to get divorced.* No way.

"You will marry three times." What? No. No. I can't.

"You will be a very successful businesswoman." That sounds better, but the whole thing is confusing. I wonder how Adnan plays into my future. Would he be one of my divorces? Would we have children?

✦

To make things even more bizarre, I feel a presence in my Glendale duplex. My friends feel it too. I feel like I'm being watched, and sometimes chased. It's terrifying. Furniture and objects move while I am away. This also happens at my friend's place upstairs.

The bathroom is the scariest, though. One time in the shower, it feels like something jumps on my back, claws digging into my shoulders. The worst is when I wake suddenly one night to a dark, shadowy presence in the doorway of my bedroom. I feel it jump on me, and I can't get out of the bed; it is pinning me down. I can't reach the phone to call for help. I even call out to God, but it still doesn't leave. Finally, after what feels like an hour, it leaves and I run upstairs to Claire's place.

I don't know if it is the paranormal. Maybe it is a lucid dream, where overexhausted people can have nightmares sometimes, even

during the day, that feel so real it's hard to tell dream from reality. I
have no idea. My mind is a mess. I try to hide my insanity.

The quiet, calm voice I heard in Paris is nowhere to be found.
All I have is panic, anxiety, and paranoia. I don't tell anyone, afraid
they may have me locked up in a mental hospital.

◆

During my months-long search, the days become a ridiculous mix
of opposing activities. My hair and makeup are done on a shoot
where I'm made up to be the epitome of fresh-faced, all-American
beauty—which is totally ironic.

Later, I go fabric shopping for school, near Skid Row, where I
walk among homeless people with my shoot makeup caked on. The
makeup gets more intense as the day wears on while the face powder
wears off, so I look like a clown. Early evenings, I'm in martial arts
class sparring, punching, and kicking. Late at night, I dance with
friends at El Paso Cantina and snort cocaine. I read my friends'
palms, which is a great party trick. I drive to Culver City two nights
a week for French class.

On weekends, I'm decked out in diamonds and couture, dining
with ambassadors and sheiks, and indulging in sex and cocaine with
Adnan.

I gravely underestimated the amount of work FIDM would be.
It ramps up, and the workload grows each week. In flat-pattern
class, I learn how to make patterns for shirts, skirts, pants, dresses,
and jackets. In draping class, my favorite, I pin fabric onto a life-size
dress form, sculpting the fabric any way my creativity takes me. My
fashion illustration class teaches me to take the ideas in my mind
and get them down on paper. I learn to do fancy illustrations, shad-
ing with watercolor and India ink, and also the more mechanical-
type production sketches used in manufacturing.

Most nights, after returning home from my various activities, I
sit at my sewing machine, where I struggle to sew yards and yards

of circular ruffles onto a dress, or engineer each different type of pocket that goes into fine men's tailoring, snorting coke till four in the morning to stay awake and focused. The time flies by because I love what I'm doing, but I'm burning myself out entirely. I think it's clear I am about to hit a wall.

I have no idea how to care for myself or protect my own sanity and soul. I am doing drugs, reading palms, seeing a psychic and a hypnotherapist, studying five different religions at the same time, learning martial arts, studying French, modeling, attending fashion design school, going out dancing several nights a week, suffering with an eating disorder, and spending my weekends living in the harem of one of the world's most powerful men. How could I possibly be confused?

Mediterranean Sea, summer 1980

LISTENING FOR GOD

October 1981

I manage to survive nine months of this insanity. I wear my mask. I show up, dress up, go out, and perform each role that I'm expected to. I keep going—until one night I become so weak and confused that I simply cannot move off my living room floor. I am numb and totally empty inside.

There is no more reserve strength to draw from. No possible adrenaline rushes left. Every single bit has been spent. Right then and there, on my back on my living room floor, I surrender. I raise my arm to the sky whispering, "Help me. . . ." I have no idea if God exists, but I have nowhere else to go.

I don't think God will answer me.

I go about my life the way I have been—doing my many varied daily activities. Yet, as I'm driving on the freeway to my next appointment with the hypnotherapist, I hear an unexpected voice. A strong, peaceful voice inside me says, *Jill, you don't need the hypnotherapist. You have Me.* It's simple and profound and I listen. I cancel my session.

I go home and compulsively pick up the phone to call my psychic. As I nervously dial, I hear the voice speak again. *You have Me. You don't need the psychic.* I set the phone down. Each time this happens, my heart overflows with love and some crazy euphoric peace. I know it sounds weird, but that's how it feels.

After exactly three weeks' time, my mind becomes completely still and peaceful. After living through those terrible months with my mind in chaos, peace feels utterly shocking. Love begins to well up inside me like I'm gonna overflow. It's absolutely surreal and beautiful. I feel connected to the source of peace and love, and I never want it to stop.

I find an apartment in Downey and move from the haunted duplex. While I pack, I try to simplify my life and throw out all my new spiritual books.

All this boiling down of my life to the bare necessities makes me wonder if I really want a couture house in Paris after all. Adnan may be disappointed in me, but I can't be owned by the business. I desperately need peace to survive. I need my personal life. I want freedom and time to reflect. Just like modeling, designing in a couture house could swallow me up. I don't think I want it anymore. I continue packing and move my few things into the apartment in Downey.

With humility and deep gratitude, I go to Penny's church to thank God for my new state of peace. I'm so overwhelmed that I'm shaking. I sit in a pew, bowing with my head over my knees with tears dripping on the floor. All I can do is whisper over and over, "Thank you, thank you. . . ." The pastor says something about how we are slaves to the things of this world, and how only God can break the chains and set us free. I can relate.

The other churchgoers probably think I look like a hooker in my miniskirt, thigh-high boots, diamond jewelry, and puffy, white-fox-fur coat, but I don't care because my heart soars with freedom and overflows with love.

Hanging on to my inner peace is my new number one priority. School is two. Adnan's got to be three.

Wearing Marina Rossi, Los Angeles, 1987

A CABINET OF DRAWERS

People compare FIDM to medical school, and it's getting more intense as time goes on.

It's harder and harder to make time for Adnan, and there's no way I can travel the world with him like he wants. But I need him. When I'm wrapped up in his arms, I feel safe, loved, and protected.

He's got creative answers to all my problems and so much wisdom about life. He calms me down, grounds me, and encourages me to follow my dreams. Then he worms his way into my brain and loves me inside and out. I never think of myself as replaceable.

A year and a half into our relationship, I have superiority as the number one pleasure wife. I never see any of the other wives I had met early on. It looks like they've moved on.

Whenever we're alone, he keeps saying, "Stay with me forever. You'll be the richest woman in the world. Don't you want to be the richest woman in the world?" What I secretly yearn for though is to be in a monogamous relationship with him, where it's just the two of us. I want a commitment that makes it clear I'm more special to him than his harem. I even hope he'll propose.

There's a rumor in the entourage that Adnan is looking to marry a second legal wife and, naturally, it will be me. If we marry, I wonder if he could give up the harem? After I graduate, I can work from

Paris, designing in the atelier that Adnan will fund for me. We could live in Paris full-time, except for his business travels, of course. Only he and I know I rejected the twenty-carat diamond ring he tried to give me in Kenya.

However, now that I'm used to seeing them on Lamia and Ines, I want a big diamond statement ring that sets me apart from all the other girls, a public declaration of his love. Because I am not capable of actually asking for what I really want in a relationship, I play it cool and act like I'm just fine with things how they are. But I'm not.

Two dozen of us are driven to the MGM Grand, where the ballroom's crystal chandeliers are sparkling and a full orchestra is playing classical music. I am seated directly across from Adnan in the center of the long table, where we sip champagne and make toasts. Adnan is totally focused on me tonight, even more than usual. He leans into the table, talking and flirting with me. Then he takes a handwritten note from his jacket and recites a poem to me. He disappears for a minute and returns with a violinist. They come over to my chair and he takes my hand. "Dance with me. I've written you a song."

We waltz together as the violinist plays, and he sings his poem to me. Photographers crazily click their cameras at us. We leave the party and return to the Dunes, where his bedroom is filled with soft music and candles. We indulge in each other.

He goes to his safe to get something, and jumps back in bed holding a red ring box. Oh my god, this is really happening! He opens the box and slips the ring on my wedding finger. But when I see the ring, my heart drops. This is not a ring Adnan would propose with. It's a small band with a gold heart and arrow of tiny diamonds. I try to act grateful, but I'm devastated.

Instead of saying, "Fuck the harem, Adnan, marry me!" I keep my emotions in check. Then I attack him. "How can you make love to all these women? How can you say you love me, and then make love to them?"

He is totally caught off guard. He smiles nervously, pointing to his furry, naked chest saying, "My heart is like a cabinet with many drawers. When I'm with you, I open that drawer and enjoy our love." He demonstrates like he's pulling out a drawer from his chest. "When I'm with someone else, I open a different drawer." He points to a different spot.

This heart of cabinets sounds ridiculous to me. "I don't understand how you can divide your heart into drawers! I could never do that. I don't get it and I don't like it."

He gets defensive. "I told you not to fall in love with me from the beginning. I told you to wait for a younger man. I'm too old for you."

"You're not too old for me, and how could I possibly spend all this time with you, making love to you, and not be in love with you?" I break down crying. "Maybe if we were together more," I whimper.

"I want you to be with me all the time! Travel on the boat with me. But you have school! You made it clear you have to work and that's your choice, not mine."

I can't control my tears. He embraces my whole body, saying, "I love you," and then, "Don't you need anything? Can't I buy you a house near school? Do you need a new car? What kind of car do you drive anyway?" He goes to his safe again.

"I drive a 1970 Ford Fairlane 500. I don't need a car," I whimper, crying and sniffling.

The safe is piled halfway up with stacks of money. He grabs a stack. "Here," he says, handing me $10,000 in hundreds. "Use it to buy makeup and clothes—things girls need."

"I don't need this. You already paid for school."

"Please take it. I insist."

For the rest of the weekend, I shove my hurt feelings down hard, numbing them with cocaine and sex.

A few nights later, Dominic takes a group of six or so potential pleasure wives to dinner and a Paul Anka concert. I'm still confused and upset and feel like I want to climb the walls, so I go along. I sit in a booth with all these girls, judging them, knowing the only reason they're here is for money. I feel like a babysitter and they're all kissing my ass, knowing I'm his number one.

During the concert, one of the girls wants to show me a ring Adnan has given her. It's dark in the concert hall, so she holds her finger in my face. I take her hand, pulling it to the candlelight to look. It's the same exact damn heart ring he just gave me. He must have bought them in bulk.

My heart pounds so hard I can hear it. We all go backstage to meet the singer. I can't wait to get back to my room.

The next morning I get up, do some floor exercises, and hit the homework. I sit in my bed, studying for a test in flat-pattern terminology. Afterward, I order a crab salad from the chef and start packing for my trip back. I shower and put on a white peasant blouse, shorts, and espadrilles.

I sit on the couch—my crab salad on the mirrored coffee table—and turn on the news. When I lean over to take a bite, the plate turns bright red. Blood is gushing from my nose. The dry desert air plus air-conditioning and cocaine are a bad combination.

I run to the bathroom, put a wet cloth over my nose, and hold my head back. Blood runs down my throat. It's a bad one, but it's time for my flight. I wet another cloth and bring it with me, pushing it against my nose. I grab my bags and rush over the little bridge that crosses the stream in my room, and out to the elevator.

Downstairs, I hurry through the casino. I jump in the back of the limo with the blood-soaked cloth over my face. Everyone stares at me as I get in. I know they think I'm a hooker. This is the last limo I take. I'm switching to incognito rent-a-cars.

After the airport, the flight, and the freeway, I drop my bags just inside my door and fall on my knees. I beg God to help me stop doing coke. I dump the leftover powder in the toilet and flush it.

Trying out for Revlon, Hollywood, 1982

RIBBON PURSES

Las Vegas

The perfect illusion and glamorous facade of Adnan's world is cracking. The world that once felt like a family to me now feels cold and cutthroat. His sparkling perfect and luxurious life surrounded by his kids and a sophisticated, intelligent entourage has morphed into a stripped-down, cheap, sad version of itself.

Ines and Lamia, the Mother Queens, are gone. The only kid I see of Adnan's is Mohammed, and that's becoming rare. Everyone has left to settle in London, New York, or Santa Barbara. Who could blame them? A Vegas hotel isn't a place to raise a family. Even Bob Shaheen and Keith are gone. Now it's just AK, Dominic, and me.

At the same time, the multiple pleasure wives that Adnan told me about in Spain are becoming more common and all too real. In the beginning it was always just Adnan and me, and if I saw another pleasure wife, it was only one at a time and she was always well educated and elegant. Yet, classy girls studying to be doctors are no longer the type he's entertaining. Now, when I go to Vegas, I meet a whole group of new and pathetic girls—sometimes I meet eight new women on one trip. It's depressingly obvious they are here to exchange sex for money—and most are addicted to cocaine.

I'm embarrassed to be seen with them because of the way they act. They flaunt their newfound wealth, jewels, and Paris Couture. In the middle of a formal dinner with Arab and American politicians, a new girl named Kristy pops out of her chair, obviously high, spinning in circles around the room, screaming, "If only my friends could see me now!" I'm serious.

As I study each woman around the table, not all are as blatant as Kristy, but they all look desperate, hungry, and lost, like they can't find another way to survive besides selling their bodies for sex. They've got no backup plan or career path. Surrounded by all these girls, I start calculating the numbers. If she sleeps with ten guys, and he has slept with twenty girls, then she sleeps with Adnan, then I sleep with Adnan, how many people's germs am I sharing?! I feel troubled, conflicted, and scared. AIDS is spreading and I don't want to get it.

A girl named Amber asks me to come to her hotel room. She sits on the floor in front of her closet and starts showing me all of her little handwoven rainbow-colored, satin ribbon purses she has made. They're pretty, but she says, "All I want is enough money to keep me in cocaine so I can keep designing my purses. Will you talk to AK about it for me and ask him to fund me in my purse business?" She's serious and it's so sad. She has no idea how the fashion business works. She can't make a living doing this. Money for cocaine so she can make ribbon purses—that's her business plan?

These lost girls make me feel so sad. Yet, after I think about it, and it sinks in, my sadness turns into action. I decide to use these women as my inspiration. I become more committed than ever to succeed in school and build a strong career. I'm not going to wind up depending on a man for money.

Paris photo studio on the Seine, 1980

DRESS-UP DOLL

Neiman Marcus, Las Vegas

Adnan asks me to go buy some new dresses. This means Neiman Marcus and Paris Couture. I used to be enamored with couture, but now it feels like a work uniform. I go anyway. As I ride the escalator up, all I can think about is how much homework I have back home. I reach the couture department and come to a dead stop.

Suddenly, I don't want any more dresses. My mind travels back to my high school days, when I bought just a simple T-shirt and felt so excited about it and appreciated it so much.

It hits me that the reason I don't want any of these expensive dresses is because I'm paying with Adnan's money, not my own hard-earned cash. I force myself over to the rack of dresses. A saleslady comes over.

"Can I help you, miss?"

"No, thanks. I'm okay." She has no idea what's going on inside me. I feel repulsed by the dresses. They're worse than empty. I walk away. I negotiate with myself that I'm here on assignment. Then, it hits me that all I'm doing is buying a dress to play a role. This isn't really me. I'm just Adnan's dress-up doll. I'm a table decoration for his fancy business dinners.

I walk over to the rack one more time, determined to get the job done and get out of there. I quickly grab a Valentino—black silk, covered in ruffles, with a purple satin bow at the waist—and hand it to the saleslady. "Charge it to Adnan Khashoggi, please."

I return to the hotel in a mental fog and put the dress in the closet, still confused, when fast knocking at my door disrupts my thoughts. I open it to Dominic in a white *thaub*, using the cane he needs when his back hurts.

"Oh hi, come on in. I just got back from shopping. What are you . . ." He pushes the door open and hobbles in. Something is majorly off. I've never seen him like this. He looks druggy and woozy. He reaches out for a hug, drops his cane and grabs on to me, forcing his mouth on mine, trying to kiss me.

"I've wanted to do this for so long! Come here, don't fight me."

"Stop it!" I shake my head back and forth trying to avoid his mouth. He grabs my blouse, ripping it off my shoulders. "What are you doing?! Get outta here!" I wedge my elbows in between us, but he hangs on, and we fall to the floor with him on top.

"I love your beautiful ass. . . . Do you know how long I've been wanting to do this?"

"Stop it, Dominic!" My martial-arts moves pop into my head, and I get out from under him and kick him away.

"Ouuuchhh!" He curls up on the floor.

"Get out!" I yell.

"I'm gonna have you," he growls, looking possessed. He gets on his hands and knees, then onto his feet, grabs his cane, and limps out. I pull my blouse up, wondering if I should tell Adnan or Ines. We've come a long way from our little manners class.

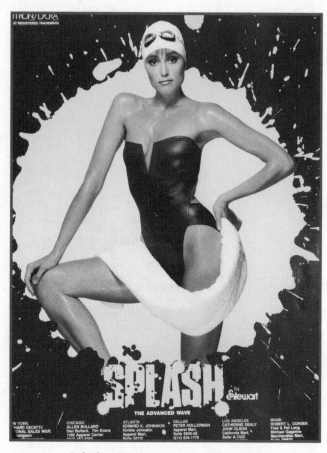

Splash swimwear, Los Angeles, 1984

THE BLACK NOTEBOOK

The Dunes Hotel, Las Vegas

Adnan and I are working peacefully at a small round table in his office. We're both wearing white *thaubs*. He works on legal documents while I'm doing fashion illustrations.

Dominic bursts into the room with a big manila envelope and a black notebook. "Hey, Chief, I've got this week's clippings." He opens the envelope and spreads the perfectly cut newspaper articles on the table. They're from all over the world and all on Adnan. We each pick up a pile and read a few. Some are about his rumored multibillion-dollar divorce. Others are about arms sales. Then Dominic holds up the black notebook. "Remember the agency I was telling you about? Lots of beauties in here, take a look at this one." He points, showing Adnan. They're much more interested in this than the news clippings.

My pulse skyrockets. I try to act like I'm focused on my drawings, dipping my fountain pen into the black inkwell, but I'm shocked at what's happening. The pages in the notebook are filled with photographs of women. Some are modeling composites like I had, and some are black-and-white glossies—head shots and body shots—just like the kind I'd seen on the walls of the pimp's house in Beverly Hills that my first agent, Miriam, had sent me to.

"Yes . . . let's see." Adnan takes the notebook from Dominic, and they browse together.

"What about Julianne? What's she like?" Adnan asks, pointing.

"She's a good girl. She's in the fifty-K range. These in the back are thirty-five K for an introduction," Dominic says.

What the fuck? I stop pretending not to be paying attention. "Do you always do this?" I ask, stunned.

"Do what?" Adnan says defensively.

"Pick girls out of a notebook!" I take a deep breath. "This isn't how you met me, is it?" They look at each other with raised eyebrows. "Did you pick me out of a book?" They giggle. My face feels like it's on fire, and my mind races back to Monte Carlo and the pirate party. Dominic was there. Pepper had brought me there—for free! I knew something was up!

Back then, I never would have dreamt that it had all been orchestrated precisely for that purpose: so Adnan could meet fresh-faced, non-sleazy models from America and Europe. I naïvely took all of them at face value, unaware that these people had motives, secrets, and agendas. And that everyone's agendas wove like a pyramid, up to the king—Adnan. Everyone worked for him. I assumed it was all about integrity, love, and friendship and thought they actually liked me. But no, I was a commodity.

I look at Adnan. "So, why do you need Dominic to find girls for you? Can't you meet them yourself?" I'm shaking and trying not to let them know it.

"And how would I do that? Do you have any ideas?" He stands up. Dominic backs up.

"I don't know—ask them out at restaurants or in stores." I stand too.

"You know I can't be in public. I can't just go up to strangers and ask them out. I have to know their backgrounds. Besides, Dominic is better-looking." They laugh.

"All the girls have to pass security clearance, Jill, you know that,"

Dominic says, standing with his ankles crossed, leaning against a console a few feet away.

"I need to hear this from you, Adnan." I look straight at him with my arms crossed.

Always charming, and with me usually wrapped around his finger, he says, "It doesn't matter now, does it? We're together. That's what's important." He hugs me and kisses my cheek. I put my arm around him for a split second, then pull it away and start packing up my homework while they continue shopping for girls.

My mind is spun. So he can't go around in public? That's evidently Dominic's job. Were Dominic and Pepper working together to find girls? Did Pepper show him photos of me? Did he pay Pepper to meet me? What about the girls in the black notebook? Were they offered money to sleep with him? Or are they being set up without knowing? Do they know who he is? Are they hookers? I'm different, right? I'm not a hooker. I don't even want his money.

The school tuition was generous, but it's to help me stand on my own two feet and not depend on anybody. The only reason I'm here is because I love him. Maybe he manipulated it all, but I fell in love with him all on my own. No one paid me to make love to him.

I survive the weekend's business dinners and sex with Adnan, seriously shoving my hurt feelings down as deep as they will go. I mask my pain, while I try to gather my thoughts about what transpired. Massages and candlelit bubble baths help me appear somewhat calm. Underneath, however, my mind is ready to implode.

I leave on Sunday, just before sunset. The Vegas airport slot machine bells ring directly into my brain while the cigarette smoke makes my head throb. Images of me stuffed in a plastic sleeve and bound in a black notebook among other Paris models torment my mind.

I've got to hold it together. I have a shoot for *Teen* magazine tomorrow and a school project due. As the plane ascends over the quiet, still desert, I stare at the serene pink-and-orange sky. Yet I feel like I'm in a straitjacket, though. My chest is tight and it's hard to breathe. This is not my idea of freedom.

I don't remember paying for parking at Lot C. I don't remember driving the freeway home. My mind has been sliced into a million pieces. Back in my Downey bedroom, I jump into work, draping and pinning pink satin onto my dress form. I need eight pattern pieces for the bodice, plus lining, and three for the skirt.

I do a strapless sweetheart neck and fold pleats in the front skirt. I add pockets because I love pockets. After a couple of hours of pinning fabric to the dress form with my tiny silver pins, I'm finally calm. I make a center slit in the back of the skirt below the zipper and cut all the pieces along the lines where the seams will go. I sew white lace on the top, hem, and back slit. I talk to God about everything while I sew late into the night—with no cocaine now.

It's good to be home safe in my own apartment bedroom, working. With my mind engrossed creatively, peace floods in, washing everything else away. I fill the princess seams with stiff boning to hold up the strapless bodice. I try it on and it fits perfectly. It's kind of Marilyn Monroe tacky, but I love it.

◆

In the morning, I stop at the Chinese drive-through donut shop on the way to the freeway. I reach Santa Monica Boulevard, where all the young boys are out, just like every morning. They sit like tiny skeletons on bus benches or at traffic lights, waiting for their next trick. Most of them are sick. They have sores and lesions on their necks and faces from AIDS. I pull into the farmers' market parking lot in West Hollywood where I'm supposed to shoot, and all I can think about are those sick young boys.

My mind bounces back to the dinner table of high-priced hookers and the black notebook Adnan and Dominic were looking through. Do I have AIDS? I could easily have AIDS. Adnan never uses protection with me. And just like the boat driver knowing about the sharks but dropping me in the ocean anyway, Adnan isn't protecting me; he's putting me in danger. I can't be his lover.

Jane from *Teen* rushes me into hair and makeup. I pose, biting into a peach in front of a fruit cart, with my mind on the notebook. I change into a dress and pose on the steps of a yellow school bus, holding a fake stack of schoolbooks. As the camera flashes I smile, wondering exactly how many women he's slept with and how many people I have been exposed to sexually. After the shoot, I jump on the Santa Monica Freeway and head downtown to my sewing class.

After school, I throw my beach towel in my car and head to the boat docks in Long Beach. I spread my towel on the dock and lie faceup, to the sun, so the hot rays melt me like honey into the dock's hardwood boards. I hear the water lap beneath the dock.

Focused on the sound of the water, I clear my mind of everything. Every thought I have comes into focus, then passes on. I pray. I give thanks for everything I can think of. Then I turn over on my stomach and hang my head over the white rubber edging of the dock. I look for fish, and check out the shiny black mussels attached to the pylons. Bright green seaweed that grows between the shells moves like wet hair with the water.

I think about nature and how miraculous salt water is. Nature brings me peace. A boater drives by. We wave to each other. I go back to contemplating the ocean life beneath me. Ever since I was small, boat docks have brought me peace. With the dock gently bobbing up and down, I feel like I'm lying on the surface of the water.

A harsh, disruptive thought shoots into my head: *Why does the issue of women being looked at as sex objects seem to follow me around?*

A series of pictures and memories flash around in my mind: *Playboy* centerfolds, Adnan's women, modeling jobs for sex, men pushing themselves on me. I want to be valued for my mind, talent, creativity, personality, humor, and heart. I want to be seen as a real person with compassion and empathy. I want respect.

Mediterranean Sea, summer 1980

MY PINK DRESS

February 1982, LAX to Vegas

Winter passes and I don't feel as connected to Adnan. There's a huge, empty space in my heart. Even if I won't sleep with him, I still love him. He wants me to drop everything and come see him, but I can't. He doesn't understand how much work I have. He's not used to that, I guess. All the other girls come running anytime because they want his money.

I begin seeing a guy my age in November, and when we finally have sex, it stirs up conflicting feelings and I start comparing him with Adnan. I love the simplicity of life with my new, non-wealthy man, yet miss Adnan's sophistication. I love being monogamous for sure. I know I can't take the harem anymore. My new guy has plenty of time for me, almost too much time, in fact. I don't even know if I even want a boyfriend. I just want to be free to pursue my own dreams.

Yet, I really miss Adnan.

By February, my heart aches for Adnan so much that I'm willing to meet him anywhere in the world just to see him. I know I can't be romantic with him. I don't know what our arrangement will be, but I still want him in my life and need to talk with him to figure out what we should do next.

In February 1982, Adnan's limo takes me to the stairway of his new DC-8 at LAX. (He paid $31 million for it and spent $9 million redesigning it.) It is like a small three-bedroom house with seat belts on the beds.

"Hello, darling." Adnan reaches for me as I board, hugging me, kissing my lips. When I see his sweet face, I remember how much I love him. If he told me he'd give up his harem, I'd be wrapped around his finger again. But I don't ask him to. I don't tell people how to run their lives. He leads me to seats that face each other where we can talk. "You need to wear your seat belt for takeoff. We have to obey the rules, you know." He laughs.

"The plane's beautiful. It's great to see you. I really missed you. My life's been a little nuts lately," I say.

"I missed you too. I don't think we've ever been away from each other this long. What's it been, four months?" he says.

"Yeah. That was a long time." I am so happy to be alone with him. The chef brings us mineral water with lemon, salmon, caviar on toast, and fruit.

"So, are you dating anyone?" he says, timidly.

"What? Boy, you get right to it, don't you?" I laugh.

"Well, are you? I haven't seen you since October, and I figured you had met someone."

"Well, I did, but that's not why I haven't come to see you. School is crazy! It's so much work. Students are dropping out every week because it's so hard."

"Tell me about this man. How old is he? Is he Arab like me?"

"It's no big deal, really. I'm not sure about him at all. I don't have much time to see him with school and he's kind of needy—kind of the opposite of you." We laugh.

"How old is he?"

"He's twenty-four and no, he's not Arab. He's an American mix of everything—you know how it is."

"What does he do for work?"

"He's an electrician."

"Where does he live?" Adnan is acting jealous. He had never had to deal with me being with another man. He leans in over the table. "Are you in love with him?"

"No. I don't know. I like him, but it's only been like four months."

Then he switches to father mode. "Does he come from a good family?"

"They seem fine. He's sweet, and I actually get to see him." I poke at Adnan again, raising my eyebrows and cocking my head. "It seems like you're traveling a lot more now."

"Yes, I've gotten busier." Then he comes back with his usual line, "But if you weren't in school, you could come with me everywhere." His initial shock seems to be wearing off, and what I am telling him seems to register. "Are you saying you want to leave me?"

"No," I cry. "I don't know. I don't know what to do. This is so hard."

"Let me know what you decide," he says. "We'll need to settle all the financial details. Remember our contract? If you decide to leave, you can always come back, you know."

"Okay." My heart aches. I don't want to leave. He feels like family. I'm closer to him than anyone, but how can it work?

"How's school?"

"It's so much work! But I love it. I'm so thankful for your help. But yeah, it's super intense. If it were easier, I'd be seeing you a lot more."

"I understand. It's good you're following your passion. It's wonderful to do what you love. Are you still modeling?"

"No. I don't have a lot of time, so just when it fits around school."

We touch down in Las Vegas and are driven to the Dunes. I have no idea that this will be the last time he and I will be alone. "I'll be away tonight, but I'll be back tomorrow and I'll see you then. We need to talk about our new arrangement," he says.

✦

I go to my suite and unpack. After writing in my journal, I decide to go swimming in the roof pool. I take off all my clothes, wrap myself in a white terry robe, and head up to the roof. As the elevator slides open, I see that I'm not alone. A young, nude girl is tanning on a chaise longue. Her perfect olive skin glistens with tanning oil. She looks exactly like me except shorter and younger. Have I been replaced?

"Hi, I'm Jill, how's it going?" I pull off my robe and lie naked on the chaise next to hers. The sun is intense, not a cloud in the sky.

"It's goin' good. I'm Renée. Are you a friend of Adnan's?"

"Yeah, are you?"

"Yeah, I mean, I just met him a couple weeks ago. He's nice, huh?" She looks barely eighteen.

"Yes, he is nice." I put my sunglasses on so I can check out her body. Am I too old for him now that I'm twenty-two? We lie baking in the sweltering desert sun. I get in the pool and start swimming.

"Do you have another boyfriend?" she asks.

"There's a guy I date back home. But I don't know if I would call him boyfriend material. How about you?"

"Yeah, I have a boyfriend in San Francisco. He's thirty-six. I like older guys. He told me I should go out with Adnan."

"So, your boyfriend's not jealous?" I see right through this bitch. I'm instantly protective of Adnan.

"No, he even drove me to the airport. He thinks it's good for my future."

Manipulative little shit. "The guy I see is really jealous of Adnan. It's driving him crazy that I'm here." I can't take it anymore. My insides are churning. I get out and dry off.

"Well, I have homework to do, so I'll see you later." I go back to my room.

I work on sketches for my collection design class. However, the bulk of the work I need to do is at home. I couldn't cart my sewing machine, pattern table, and dress form all the way to Vegas. I had no idea Adnan would be gone my first night here. I came to see him, not sit in a hotel room. The next day after lunch, I call Dominic, sure that Adnan would be here now.

"Dominic, where's Adnan? Is he back?"

"No, he's still out of the country. He should be back tonight."

My resentment grows by the hour. I'm angry with myself for putting him ahead of everything I need to do, just to be left in this stupid room. Our relationship isn't a two-way street. It's always worked around his schedule, not mine.

When he picked me up in his plane, I assumed he had arranged his schedule to see me—not just drop me in Vegas and leave the country. He's being so unfair! I can't put my life on hold like this. He really doesn't understand that I have work to do. I pace around the room, wondering what the hell to do with my life and with Adnan. The thing that pisses me off the most is that I am not in control of anything—and I hate that feeling!

I do everything I can think of to keep from going crazy. I lie on the floor and I do leg exercises and crunches. I set my work up on the couch and coffee table and study for my marketing exam. I light all the vanilla candles and try to calm down in a bubble bath. I get in bed, write in my diary, and pray. I get back up, walk back and forth in front of the window, and gaze out at the desert, like a caged animal. At midnight, I take another bubble bath and finally get to sleep around 1 A.M.

At 2 A.M., my phone startles me awake, rattling my nerves. I answer to Dominic shouting, "It's time for dinner! He's here!"

"Oh my god, Dominic, I'm sleeping. Not now, please, I really need to sleep."

"You need to be at this dinner, Jill. You gotta get up. Don't go back to sleep!"

"I've been waiting for him for two days, and now it's past midnight!" I plea.

Dominic says authoritatively, "Get dressed and meet us in the salon." His tone reminds me of my dad, which doesn't go over well.

So Adnan arrives from some other time zone and wants to throw a dinner party in the middle of the night—convenient for him, but not for me. Still, I know the drill. I have to drag myself out of bed and dress in couture. I throw my leg over the side of the bed and slide down till my knee hits the floor, followed by the rest of my body. I sit up on my carpeted bed pedestal, illuminated by a narrow tube of tiny purple lights, and put my head between my knees. Then I stand up and stomp to the bathroom.

Instead of wearing my hair straight down, I rat it up and out as big as I can, just like Nicole does when we go out dancing. I cover it in hair spray. Leaning into the mirror, I brush pink, iridescent eye shadow over my lids and line my eyes with bright blue sparkly liner. Thick mascara and glossy, hot-pink lips finish it off. This is a look I only use at home with my friends, never with Adnan.

I turn to the closet, pondering my options. Let's see . . . conservative, black, floor-length Lanvin or Dior, or the pink bustier dress I made for school. Fuck it. I grab the hot-pink dress and look at it, smiling. I step in and zip it up. My boobs spill out the top a little, but whatever. The lower half of the dress is just as tight, with a lace-trimmed slit in back. I pull on white nylons, step into my white pumps, and lean in to the mirror as I put on gold hoop earrings. This is me. I'm not his fucking dress-up doll.

I meet everyone in Adnan's salon. When he walks in and sees me, he's in shock. Adnan, Renée, and I pile into his silver bullet-proof limo. This is a new arrangement, though. I have never shared a car with him and another girl. They sit together, facing forward, and I sit across from them, facing backward. He can't believe the way I look and keeps staring at me, giggling. She looks smug and full of herself, staring across at me. I feel like saying, *You don't know what you're getting into, you little brat. You're playing with fire, baby girl.*

Adnan says, "Jill, doesn't Renée look beautiful tonight? Don't you love her dress?" *Why don't you just stab me, AK?* I think.

"She looks beautiful," I reply, seething, trying to act happy.

"And what are you wearing?" he asks.

"Oh, I made it for an assignment at school, where we had to design a dress with princess seams and boning." I point out all the details, as if they really care.

"Well, the only thing I can say about it is it's nice that you made it by hand." His disapproval is obvious, but he manages to get his point across without being mean.

About thirty people are gathered in the private dining room of a dimly lit restaurant. The table is filled with men, except for Renée and me. Dominic is there, playing with a small tape recorder in his pocket, for whatever reason. Adnan's son Mohammed sits directly across from Adnan in the senior position. I sit on Adnan's right.

The purpose of this meeting becomes clear fairly quickly. Hollywood wants money. Producers and directors around the long table begin pitching their film projects, while Adnan's entourage of men bicker and compete over who has the coolest James Bond–type gadgets.

Dominic's on my right, boasting about evidence he has on his mini tape recorder, trying to intimidate the other men. A man at the end of the table flashes a personal check from his jacket pocket and slides it back in, winking. Adnan begins his sarcastic and strategic banter. He's ready to play all these people. And they won't even know they've been played.

The dinner goes on and on. At some point, Adnan leans into the table and teasingly threatens his son Mohammed, "You better make a move on Brooke Shields soon, or I will."

I don't see this playful threat to date another, way-too-young, beautiful girl as fun banter, though. His threat triggers my anger. Adnan's womanizing is hurting me, and I don't want it to hurt his son too. My pulse skyrockets, and I feel the overwhelming urge to protect Mohammed. I jump down Adnan's throat. "Why don't you leave him alone? He told me he's not ready for a relationship yet, and you're trying to make him just like you are." I lean into him, emphasizing the "you." I may have even pointed my finger.

Mohammed's eyes go huge. Everyone around the table within earshot suddenly gets quiet and looks at us. No one talks to Adnan like that. Ever.

I'd had it. "Excuse me." I get up to go to the ladies' room, adjusting my dress over my hips as I squeeze out between the chairs. My blood is boiling and my face feels hot. I don't even see what's in front of me. As I march across the restaurant to the ladies' room, I seethe over Adnan trying to turn Mohammed into a womanizer.

I enter the restroom stall, peel my white nylons over my hips, and try to calm down so I can pee. I hear water running. I hadn't noticed anyone when I came in. When I come out of the stall, a petite, older black woman in a simple uniform stands near the sink. Yet, there's something different about her. She is glowing. She has a bright aura around her, and she has all of my attention. Time stands still. Water runs in the sink. She had turned it on while I was in the stall, so it would be warm. I look down at the sink and wash my hands, then turn back to her. She holds out a towel for me and says kindly, "Honey, that is the prettiest dress I have ever seen." She radiates love. If angels exist, this is one. My mind is officially blown.

I hug the lady in the bathroom as tears run down my cheeks. I wipe my face and walk slowly back to the table. My mind is totally on her. She might be poor, working as a bathroom attendant, but I'd prefer life with her, under any conditions, than living with these piranhas.

Adnan stands and pulls out my chair. I sit in the center of this table, seeing it as if from above the room with a crystal-clear perspective. Twenty-five male egos are battling it out with one another. Renée is trying to look pretty and charming. Mohammed seems used to all this. Adnan clearly has the power position. With their testosterone pumping, these men grovel at his feet, using any strategy they can think of as they fight for the prize—Adnan's money. They look pathetic playing their stupid power games. I can't take it anymore. I don't want to be part of this shit. I'm done. I want out.

◆

Back home, as I'm submerged in an ungodly amount of schoolwork, Adnan calls over and over, wanting me to meet him in New York or Paris to talk about our contract and our future. But I've got final school projects and a whole collection to design. I need to make patterns, shop fabrics and trims, and sew the entire collection.

Plus, I'm planning a huge graduation fashion show for hundreds of students and over a thousand guests. I know he wants to talk about money, but I don't want his money. He still doesn't understand my need to work, and probably never will. I don't think he's ever met an independent girl like me. I want to make it on my own. And I do.

Tearing my love away from Adnan feels like surgery, like something has to be physically cut out of me in order to get over it. Sometimes I entertain the idea of designing from his ship and living in Paris so I can see him more. That can work. But his lack of monogamy will not. It's an impossible situation. I have to tear myself away from him.

We talk on the phone a few times, trying to coordinate our schedules. He wants to meet in person to discuss our parting of the ways, which probably means something financial. I just want to know that he's still my friend.

All spring, I wrestle with myself over him. I pray for help in letting him go, and healing for my heart. It's awful. He's more than a lover or a boyfriend. He's my calm, safe haven. He has all the answers and always knows what to say. I miss his sarcasm and humor. I miss all the stupid little bets we made against each other. I miss laughing with him and all the silly things we did. I miss lying in bed curled up on him, with my head tucked into his neck.

FIDM teacher Mr. Costas, June Van Dyke, and me, Los Angeles Hilton ballroom, December 18, 1982

GRADUATION

June to December 1982

Finally, by May, my heart is free from hurting over Adnan and my vision is clear. From June to December, I have graduation to focus on. In September, at the start of our last semester, our Collection Development teachers gather all of the graduating students in a room to deliver the bad news to us that FIDM will not be putting on a graduation show this year.

The show is supposed to be the vehicle that launches us into the world, where powerful fashion industry people attend looking for fresh, new designers. It's what we've worked toward throughout every week of school.

The news is devastating. Everyone is worried about getting a job. How can we land jobs without a platform to show our work? Students are either freaking out, or silently turning inward. I feel angry and seriously bummed, until my mind begins to churn. *I've been in hundreds of shows. It's not that complicated. Why should I just accept their decision? I'm not the kind of girl who gives up or takes no for an answer. I know how to run a show. Why can't I put on a show?*

I go directly to the administration office to ask if it's really true and why? The woman tells me it's the economy. The US is in the worst recession, with unemployment higher than it's been since the Great Depression. When I tell her my plan to put on a show myself, she's not happy. So unhappy in fact that she tells me that I can't use the FIDM name on anything.

Does she think it will be so bad that they'll be ashamed of it? Her comments make me even more determined. I instantly start calculating the number of guests to determine the venue size. With my count of around fifteen hundred, we need a large ballroom at a major hotel. I have a little money in the bank, since I worked as much as I could through school, so I go across the street to the hotel where my friend Benny Washington works and put a deposit on the Pacific Ballroom at the Los Angeles Hilton for December 18. They have everything we need: audio equipment, lights, a backstage area to change in, even a long catwalk.

Our Collection Development teachers can't believe I am taking this on. My teacher, Mr. Fuller, tells me to contact June Van Dyke, a well-known fashion show producer and announcer. She was the assistant to Edith Head, Hollywood's most famous costume designer. When Edith died in 1981, June inherited her personal collection of costumes. She offers to let me model Edith's most iconic costumes at our show—dresses worn in movies by Audrey Hepburn and Elizabeth Taylor. She also agrees to be our announcer at a very fair price. I am beyond thrilled.

When I tell the other students I am going to put on a show for the entire graduating class, they look at me like I'm nuts and probably don't think I can do it. But they've got nothing to lose but the price of their tickets. When I go into detail, describing the glamorous setting of the Pacific Ballroom of the Los Angeles Hilton, the lights, the catwalk, and the music, every student beams. (It was later named the Wilshire Grand Hotel; it was demolished in 2013 and has now become the tallest structure in the LA skyline: the Wilshire Grand Center.)

The mood at school goes from dreary to ecstatic elation. We

buzz around like bees, designing our collections, enduring sleepless nights, making patterns, draping on dress forms, and sewing. On top of this, we have finals in all our other classes, and by graduation we're running on fumes.

I'm so excited, nervous, and stressed before the show that I decide to fast and pray for three days. When I get hungry, I pray even more for our big day to be a huge success. I don't want to let anyone down. It's too big for me to handle, so I keep giving it to God.

◆

Since we use our friends as models, I hold a meeting to teach everyone how to walk the catwalk. "Walk in a straight line, chin up, looking straight ahead to the end of the runway. Do a spin or two, smiling at the guests along the way. If you trip, get up and keep walking. Nothing's worse than a stalled show."

I print formal invitations and we sell out the entire Pacific Ballroom. My friend John makes an authentic eighties fashion show soundtrack, and best of all we have June Van Dyke as our MC.

I feel so grateful to Adnan for paying my school tuition. I want him to come to the show and see everything I've worked so hard for. I want him to know I didn't squander the money he gave me, and I want him to be proud of me. I send an invitation to his Paris mansion at 8 Avenue Montaigne, hoping he'll come, but I don't hear back.

The week before the show, we receive bad news. Our two Collection teachers, Mr. Fuller and Mr. Costas, tell us that they are not allowed to attend. They say the administration has threatened to cut their hours if they come. I can't understand why the administration is so against our show. Are they trying to undermine us? Do they think it makes them look bad for canceling? Are they worried they will be ashamed of it? It feels like my own school is working against me. We feel alone without the support of our teachers. Because I'm not allowed to use the FIDM name on the invitations, I print, "Graduating Fashion Designers present 1983 Collections" instead.

The morning of the show, I arrive at the hotel and go straight to the ballroom to make sure everything is moving smoothly. The catering department is on the job, rolling in tables, surrounding them with chairs, and assembling the long catwalk. My friend John is setting up the music system and doing sound checks. Others are busy sound-checking the microphones at the podium. A small group of students are dressing the tables with floral centerpieces.

The room begins to explode with energy as all the students and their posses of models rush in. Then, just before the flood of guests is allowed in, we are met with a terrific surprise! Mr. Fuller and Mr. Costas—the very men who helped us shape each collection— enter the room. Risking their pay, these two elegant men rush straight backstage to greet the students and get to work. Rousing screams of joy fly out from behind the big red curtains. We worship these two men, and the fact that they came to support us after they were told not to thrills us. They're industry veterans with decades of fashion show experience, and they get right to work organizing and lining up models, checking the styling, and wishing us good luck!

June arrives holding three of Edith Head's iconic dresses for me to model. I quickly change backstage into Audrey Hepburn's little black dress from the movie *Sabrina*. The packed room of proud parents, friends, and fashion industry professionals buzzes with excitement.

As the lights go down, I take the stage and stand at the podium. "Welcome to the Fashion Institute of Design and Merchandising's graduating class of nineteen eighty-two!" Applause erupts. "I'd like to introduce Edith Head's assistant and producer, June Van Dyke!"

June takes the mic—a total professional, mixing a joyous welcome with fashion insider details and humor. John cranks up the music and we open the show with Edith Head's designs, June giving the historical details of each famous dress as I walk the catwalk. Everything is perfect.

Each designer sends their troupe of models down the runway,

flaunting their hard work and talent. They look so good it's hard to believe they're not seasoned designers and models. Each collection is met with crazy, excited applause.

The varied collections reflect the diversity and individuality of each student. One does a collection of women's business attire; another designs nude-colored silk blouses, skirts, and dresses with delicate hand beading and appliqué. Her patience is astounding. My friend Dana unveils a collection of lingerie, and Olivia does a collection of clothes in sizes 14 to 22—so rare at the time. Since I love evening gowns, I design floor-length dresses in jewel-toned satin—sapphire blue, ruby red, amethyst, black, and gold, trimmed in black raven's feathers. The silhouettes have kimono sleeves, fitted hips, and thigh-grazing slits.

Each time I walk the runway, I scan the audience for Adnan, hoping he's come to surprise me. But with each trip down the runway, my hopes fade a little more. He's not here. He is the only thing missing from this beautiful and triumphant day.

After the last collection of models walk the runway, and the house lights come back on, I go into the audience to greet friends and family. I'm electric with adrenaline. I spot two women from the school administration office in the crowd. I'm surprised and a little confused, but happy they're here. Did they have a change of heart? I walk over and say hi and thank them for coming. They say they loved the show. Somehow, I still feel like a rebel.

Designing ROXY in Paris, 1989

EPILOGUE

My little Fiat 500 is packed with teenage girls—one of them is mine. I am endlessly entertained, and curious about the issues they face. Every one of them is on their phone, checking Instagram, texting, and taking Snapchat videos. While I drive, I'm wondering how this instant access and constant speedy digestion of information will affect their lives.

"Okay, girls, frozen yogurt's gotta be quick because I gotta get back to work." They know I'm writing a book. One of them in the back seat asks, "What's your book about, Jill?"

My heart drops and I pause, wondering what to say and not to say. "Do you really wanna know?" I ask nervously.

"Yes, yes! I do! I do!" she pushes.

I try to put it in a nutshell. "Well, it's about a young girl, me, who goes to Paris to make it as a model and winds up in a harem."

"What's a harem?" they ask.

"It's where a rich Saudi Arabian man has lots of wives."

They take this in stride. Then one says, "Was he in the Illuminati?"

"How do you guys know about that?" I laugh.

"All the guys at school are obsessed with the Illuminati!"

Wow, I had no idea. "Anyway, I wasn't good at standing up for myself like I am now, so I went through a lot with agents and photographers and men. But I wasn't held hostage like in the movie *Taken*. The Arab man was honest with me from the beginning. We actually had a great relationship until I got sick of the harem. He paid my fashion design school tuition."

Stella says, "You guys know my mom started ROXY, right?" The car erupts in teenage girls screaming questions at me. . . .

"What?!"

"How did you start ROXY?!"

"Is that true, Jill?"

"Yeah, it is."

"How did you do it?" they scream.

I take a deep sigh of relief, realizing that this car full of independent, spirited, young women is far more interested in how to run a fashion company than what it's like to live in a billionaire's harem.

✦

Working and living in the fashion business for more than twenty-five years, I did everything from cutting samples to creating, designing, branding, and launching new companies. Fashion was always my big love. Fashion is an art form, and crucial in expressing our own unique personal style. It communicates who we are to the world.

You should see the looks on people's faces when they find out I was in a harem. It's so funny. But I didn't always find it funny. It took years for me to not feel ashamed when the topic came up. Yet, at fifty-seven, I no longer beat myself up over all my mistakes and character misjudgments. I now know it was part of my growth as a woman.

We all have scars. We are all wounded. Life is incredibly messy and unpredictable. Obtaining the grace and wisdom to know when to surrender and accept what life throws, or to fight like hell, can take a lifetime to learn.

I now know that no one is coming to save me. I must save myself. And if I need help, it's my responsibility to ask. It's my obligation to learn, grow, and move forward. I believe we are here to grow. I've learned and become better at setting boundaries and protecting my peace. I know how to ask for help and to keep looking until I find the information and support I need.

Life with Adnan taught me that money and success don't buy peace or happiness, and because I have a lot of personal motivation and ambition, I have to remind myself that "stuff" won't make me happy—although I love brilliant design and fine craftsmanship. Still, love, friendship, laughter, good health, being creative, working hard, and working together are the things that fill my heart up.

I believe in making bold choices and creating a life without fear. When my dreams get shattered, I remember to be grateful for what I have. Then, over time, use my imagination to create a new set of dreams and goals.

I will never understand God, but will keep praying and meditating because it gives me strength and peace. When I'm watching for it, I'll see a glimmer of heaven through the beauty of nature, a small miracle, or the love of others.

I have found that the currency of love is respect, empathy, and actively expressing our care and support of those we love. It's an action—not a passive thing. Love is alive and rises from our spirit and soul. The more we use it, the better it gets.

Today, with my children, my husband, and my amazing friends, my life is filled with love, laughter, sunshine, support, and peace.

ACKNOWLEDGMENTS

I had no idea how to write a book. I learned by writing over and over and from feedback from friends, coaches, and editors. Juliane Caillouette Noble, working with you in London gave my story structure and soul to build upon—thank you for cooking all those amazing lunches! Shea O'Hill, your understanding of what I was trying to accomplish and wise editing gave me the courage to say what I really wanted to. Christine Bronstein, you came to me when I needed you most, and you pulled out the clarifying emotions I tended to hide. Emily Han, thank you for pushing me further and developing the whole story in a deeper, more focused way. Your writing prompts are so damn good! Thank you also to Lauren Bruno, John Payne, and Sarah Stone, who coached me in the very beginning. I'm sure you rolled your eyes at my lack of skill and are surprised that I never gave up.

Thanks to Judith Curr at Atria for your wild, spirited passion for books. Thank you to Haley Weaver for holding every single production detail together with such care and professionalism. Many thanks to Diane Shanley for your brilliant copy edit! And to Albert Tang and Rodrigo Corral for the fantastic cover design. I love it!

Big thanks to Edward Ash-Milby for believing in my story all along. To my many early readers, thank you for your encouragement and steadfast strength that held me up for seven years while I wrote this book. I am grateful to Jillian Lauren, Claire Bidwell Smith, Jenny Feldon, and my Story & Soul sisters for their bravery in writing at their memoir workshop in Ojai, California. Thank you to Enliven authors for your encouragement and support. I'm so glad we have one another. I am forever grateful to my publisher, Zhena Muzyka, for her instantaneous love and belief in my story. Your wise and loving spirit is what we need more of, and I'm glad you are publishing books that heal, encourage, and enlighten. Thanks to my children, Brek, Natalie, and Stella, for pulling together and helping while I wrote. You three are my sunshine, rainbows, and unicorns, and I love you! And thank you, Jeff, my precious husband, for your constant support and love. You are a miracle, and I love you!

PERMISSIONS

Thank you to the many incredibly talented photographers that have been so kind and generous in allowing me to include their photos in this book. Below are the photographer credits alongside the page numbers of where their photographs appear. I loved working with all of you.

ABOUT THE AUTHOR

Born and raised in Los Angeles, Jill Dodd is a writer and artist. She gained recognition for bridging the worlds of men's and women's surfing as the founder and designer of ROXY, where she was the first to sponsor female surfers. Jill graduated with honors from the Fashion Institute of Design and Merchandising and spent seventeen years as an American swimwear designer. Her bestselling designs at Jag were known as much for their edgy style as for their great fit, due to her many years working as a fit model. While at Jag, she sponsored professional female volleyball players and windsurfers. At Sunsets and Blink, Jill helped to revolutionize the industry by selling bikini tops and bottoms separately. Prior to her work as a fashion designer, Jill spent ten years as a fashion model. She has appeared in *Vogue Paris, Marie Claire, Glamour, Harper's Bazaar, Mademoiselle, Teen, Cosmopolitan, Girls Magazine, New York Apparel News, Women's Wear Daily*, and many other publications while signed to Wilhelmina Models USA and Paris Planning Europe. She has acted in commercials for the Gap, Vittel, Sprite, and many others. A skilled painter, Jill joined the artist community Laguna Canyon Artists, and she had her first exhibit of paintings in Newport Beach, California, in 2002. She is currently practicing in ceramics. Jill lives with her husband and three children in Northern California. And yes, she married three times, just like Adnan's holy man said she would.

ENLIVEN™

About Our Books: We are the world's first holistic publisher for mission-driven authors. We curate, create, collaborate on, and commission sophisticated, fresh titles and voices to enhance your spiritual development, success, and wellness pursuits.

About Our Vision: Our authors are the voice of empowerment, creativity, and spirituality in the twenty-first century. You, our readers, are brilliant seekers of adventure, unexpected stories, and tools to transform yourselves and your world. Together, we are change-makers on a mission to increase literacy, uplift humanity, ignite genius, and create reasons to gather around books. We think of ourselves as instigators of soulful exchange.

Enliven Books is a new imprint from social entrepreneur and publisher Zhena Muzyka, author of *Life by the Cup*.

To explore our list of books and learn about fresh new voices in the realm of Mind-Body-Spirit, please visit us at

EnlivenBooks.com | **⑥/EnlivenBooks**